WILD TEA

This edition published by OH Editions
An imprint of the Welbeck Publishing Group
20 Mortimer Street London W1T 3JW

Text copyright © Richard Hood and Nick Moyle 2020
Design © Welbeck Non-Fiction Limited,
part of Welbeck Publishing Group Limited 2021
Cover design by James Pople

British Library Cataloguing-in-Publication data available on request.

ISBN 978-1-91431-727-9

10 9 8 7 6 5 4 3 2 1

Printed in China

DISCLAIMER

All images © Richard Hood and Nick Moyle
2020, except: © Eddison Books Ltd 2020: pages
2, 4–5, 22–23, 24, 29, 49, 53, 56, 59, 61, 62, 71,
75, 77, 81, 85, 87, 89, 91, 97, 99, 101, 103, 104,
120tl, 120bl, 120br, 121, 122, 124, 125, 126, 127,
129, 131, 132, 134, 139, 140, 143, 145, 146, 147, 148,
152, 155, 157, 161, 163, 168 / Shutterstock: page 7
ArtSyslik, 38 Sunvik, 165 mama_mia.

WILD TEA

BREW YOUR OWN INFUSIONS
FROM HOME-GROWN AND
FORAGED INGREDIENTS

NICK MOYLE AND **RICHARD HOOD**

OH EDITIONS

Contents

Foreword

Hello there, we are Nick and Rich, also known as the Two Thirsty Gardeners, and we grow and forage for things to turn into drinks. Our first book, *Brew it Yourself*, featured boozy beverages, so we thought it was time to sober up with teas for our second book. We live in Somerset, England, where the countryside is well-stocked with forageable ingredients, and we also grow whatever our lazy gardening methods allow – Nick in his garden and Rich on his allotment.

So pull up a comfortable chair, pour yourself a cup of tea, sit down and relax as we tell you all about wild tea. You could, of course, skip to the recipes and launch straight into brewing a cuppa, but there are a few things you might like to know before you do. Are you sitting comfortably? Then let us begin...

What is Wild Tea?

We use the term 'wild tea' to cover infusions and decoctions (see below) made from ingredients other than 'proper' teas that come from the *Camellia sinensis* plant (see *page 20*). These flowers, leaves, seeds, fruits and roots can be turned into a huge range of delicious drinks, usually with the same minimal effort as brewing a regular cuppa, giving you an infinite range of flavours with which to fill your pots, cups and mugs.

Lots of the ingredients featured in this book can be found in the wild, and many more can be cultivated in the wilds of your own garden (or even a pot or window box for those short on space), but for us their 'wildness' is just as much about the experimental process of deviating from familiar teas and into new taste territories.

To set you on your way, we've picked out our forty favourite wild tea ingredients, chosen not only for their great taste, but also because they're easy to grow or forage, or are so essential that we couldn't leave them out. We've also highlighted more ingredients in the Best of the Rest section, focusing on those that didn't quite make our top forty, along with some other interesting and unusual plants that have a tea-time tale to tell.

For those of you who want some inspiration for blending teas, we have a whole section on just that. We've also got some extra special tea and coffee recipes that require a bit more effort than simply infusing – these include sun teas, iced teas, bubble teas and other brewing delights.

But before all of that, we want to give you a few pointers on how to grow, forage and dry your own ingredients, and explain some of the key tea terminology so you'll be an expert in no time. Now, isn't it time for another cup of tea...?

TEAS, TISANES, INFUSIONS AND DECOCTIONS

A good cuppa comes in many guises. The term 'wild tea' encompasses all of the following tea-type drinks:

Teas: There has been some debate in the UK about whether herbal, fruit and botanical teas should technically be labelled as 'tea'. The word 'tea' comes from the common name given to *Camellia sinensis* – the 'tea plant' – so people will argue that it shouldn't be applied to drinks that are made from other ingredients. However, we think language is flexible enough to allow us to ignore this technicality and refer to all of our infusions and decoctions 'tea'.

Tisanes: The French already have a word for these drinks – *tisane*.* Although it's occasionally used in English, it sounds a bit too fancy for common folk like us to use with any confidence, so we're sticking with tea.

Infusions: In tea terms, this is the name for a drink made by pouring boiling water over your chosen ingredients and allowing them to steep in order to extract their flavours.

Decoctions: This term is used to describe drinks that have been made by simmering ingredients in boiling water. This method is used to extract flavour from items that are more reluctant to give up their goodness by infusion alone.

COFFEE AND MILK

We also have a few recipes that tell you how to make coffee and milk substitutes. Although no coffee beans or cows were involved in the making of these drinks, we will refer to them as 'coffee' and 'milk' because coming up with alternative names is just too confusing...

SHOP-BOUGHT INGREDIENTS

We find that growing or foraging for your own ingredients is part of the fun of wild tea making. But you don't have to rely on such wild ways to source the goods – rummaging around the shops is a perfectly acceptable method for gathering your tea-making bounties. Even among our forty favourite ingredients, there are a few entries that we neither grow or forage for ourselves (lemon being a notable example), but we deem them too important and tasty to ignore.

You'll be able to make a large number of these teas from ingredients found in a well-stocked supermarket, and just about every other item will be available online (particularly in dried form), so you can infuse and decoct without even leaving the house, let alone getting your fingers muddy.

If you're lucky enough to have access to a good herbalist or apothecary, then these are the ideal places to source dried ingredients. You can see and sniff (and maybe even have a nibble) before you buy and can usually get whatever amount you wish weighed out, allowing you to experiment with the flavours before stocking up on larger quantities.

HEALTH AND WELLBEING

Although many of the ingredients in this book have well-known health and wellbeing benefits, we're not medical experts and tend to take some of the more remarkable sounding claims with a large dose of scepticism. Even if, for example, you believe that blackcurrant leaves can cure aching joints, you would likely need to take the teas as regular doses over a period of time (just like prescription drugs), in which

case a little chat with your doctor first would be well advised. It is also the case that not all vitamins are water soluble, so simply dunking an ingredient in hot water won't necessarily release all of its good stuff.

We've highlighted some medical claims surrounding each of our main ingredients as they help to build a bigger picture about the reasons for their popularity, but mostly we've included ingredients for their flavour, rather than their health benefits.

Disclaimer: It's worth mentioning that, as with consuming anything, some of the ingredients featured may cause unwanted side effects, particularly if you ingest a lot of them or start to use them regularly. Anyone with an existing medical condition, or who is pregnant or breastfeeding, should be extra cautious. Some people can also have allergies to certain ingredients, so treat everything with caution. It's also worth noting that with many of our ingredients there are multiple varieties of the same species, so take extra care to check that the one you're using is safe to consume.

---

* *Just as you could argue that 'tea' should only refer to drinks made from the tea plant, you could say that 'tisane' should only refer to drinks made from barley, as the word derives from the Greek ptisane meaning 'peeled barley'. We told you language was flexible...*

Brewing Basics

Making tea is not exactly rocket science, but here are some Two Thirsty Gardener tips to ensure you get the very best from your ingredients.

HOW MUCH?

The quantities given in this book are only guidelines. You may like your tea stronger, lighter, sweeter or served any other way. Think about the many different ways people drink black tea and coffee and the same variations can be applied to wild teas. It may take several cups until you hit on your own personal preferences.

DRIED OR FRESH?

Where possible, we have indicated whether ingredients should be dried or used fresh. These are our preferences, but in the spirit of this book, we urge you to experiment. For example, we like the savoury edge that dried rose petals can bring, but you may prefer the floral sweetness of freshly picked specimens for your own herbal brews.

RELEASE THE FLAVOUR

When using fresh ingredients, some plants require a bit of encouragement to release their essential oils and flavours. To do this, give them a brief rub between the palms of your hands before dropping into your pot or cup.

WHAT TEMPERATURE?

Fully oxidized teas, such as black tea, require freshly boiled water poured at 100°C (212°F) to fully release their flavour. However, for a tip-top brew made from more delicate ingredients, such as green teas (and most of the ingredients in this book), leave your kettle to cool for a few minutes before pouring.

TEA-TIME(ING)

As a general rule, steep your concoctions for five minutes before tasting. If you feel your brew needs a bit more flavour, give it another five minutes and take another sip.

TEA-MAKING KIT

We've listed below the key items you'll need to aid you in your tea-making experiments:

INFUSERS

These devices will hold your tea ingredients in situ while they infuse, allowing the flavours to flow, but stopping particles from floating around in your chosen vessel. They come in various guises, from elaborate infuser wands to reusable silicone tea bags. Our tool of choice is the no-nonsense 'tea globe' – a stainless steel mesh ball attached to a chain for easy removal.

If you plan to prepare and serve your herbal brews on a larger scale, teapots with built-in infusers are worth a look. You can also buy thermal infuser flasks for brewing on the go. Steeping and brewing times will be a bit haphazard, but for making simple mint teas on your allotment they are just the ticket.

STRAINERS

If you choose not to follow the infuser route, it's always good practice to strain your brews before serving. Small, cup-sized ones that rest on the rim are best, but a sieve used for baking can be an effective, albeit less graceful, alternative.

STRAWS

For elegant sampling of iced teas and cold-served beverages, straws are ideal. Stainless steel ones are best for the environment, and you'll need to source some wide-bored ones if you fancy trying our Bubble Tea (see *page 162*).

CHOPPING BOARD

A concave hardwood board will help you prep without spilling your precious ingredients. Combine it with a half-moon herb chopper to rock and roll through ingredients with precision and speed.

PESTLE AND MORTAR

You'll need these to help grind up some of the more resilient ingredients. Don't forget to rest the mortar (the cup part) on a chopping board or tea towel when grinding to prevent damage to your kitchen surfaces.

DIGITAL SCALES

These are very useful for weighing incredibly light ingredients and will enable you to experiment with more nuanced mixtures.

MEASURING SPOONS

The measurements in this book are for guidance only so you don't need to get too hung up on precision, but a set of stainless steel measuring spoons is a handy kitchen ally.

SLOTTED SPOON

This is essential for high-speed stirring and for the removal of unwanted objects that would otherwise spoil your cuppa.

STERILIZATION

When making and bottling the syrups in this book, remember to sterilize your chosen receptacles carefully before use, in order to prevent unwanted cultures forming and spoiling your syrup. There are a couple of ways of doing this. You can get hold of a chemical sterilizing solution from your local chemist and follow the instructions (usually a 20-minute immersion does the trick). Or you can deploy the oven method: simply wash your bottles thoroughly in soapy water, then sit them upside down on a roasting tray in a preheated oven at 180°C (356°F) for 15 minutes.

Drying Ingredients

While some ingredients taste best fresh, many more are just as good – if not better – when dried. If you want to create blends and store teas long after their harvest season has ended, then drying them first is essential.

HOW TO DRY YOUR INGREDIENTS

There are many reasons why you might want to dry your wild tea ingredients. Besides enabling you to store them for longer, they will be easier to crumble or grind into smaller pieces, making them more suitable for infusers and homemade tea bags. Dried ingredients provide maximum blending opportunities (particularly useful when combining ingredients from different seasons) and, in many instances, drying intensifies flavour for a better tasting brew.

There are two main things that ingredients need to dry successfully: heat and air. While heat extracts the water, air circulating around the ingredients throughout the process will dry them more evenly and disperse any moisture, preventing it from building up where it's not wanted.

Successful drying can be achieved naturally by placing your ingredients somewhere warm in the open (for example, a conservatory, greenhouse or even a hot windowsill), or by using a heat source such as an oven or a specialist dehydrator. Delicate ingredients (small flowers and thin leaves) dry quickly, so the open air method is often best, while thicker leaves, fruits and roots will generally benefit from the more consistently hot temperatures provided by ovens or dehydrators. Some leaves and flowers can be dried while still on their stalks, enabling you to tie them together and suspend them, before plucking the goods off when finished.

To allow air to circulate freely, dehydrators are fitted with specially designed trays so you can leave your ingredients unattended throughout the drying process. Oven users will have to lay their ingredients out on a tray and regularly turn them to make sure they dry evenly.

To create the most flavoursome dried teas, it's best to start the process as soon as possible after picking. Always wash ingredients first and remove as much water as possible by patting with a clean towel or absorbent kitchen paper. Try to dry ingredients of a similar size and thickness to make sure everything is ready at the same time and, for larger items, slice them thinly so they will dry more evenly and in a shorter amount of time.

Items are fully dried and ready for storage when there's no moisture left in them – leaves and flowers will lose their flexibility and crumble easily, while thicker items become firm and dry and can be easily ground. The best place to store your newly dried tea-making ingredients is in a well-sealed opaque tin, jar or bag somewhere cool and dark.

DRYING CITRUS FRUITS

When drying citrus fruits, you can choose to slice the whole fruit into discs (often referred to as wheels) or just peel off and use the outer zest. The former will provide you with impressive looking discs containing all the flavours of the fruit, but this will include the bitterness of the pith, which can tarnish some delicate tea blends.

DRYING TEMPERATURES AND TIMES

We haven't included drying temperatures or times in this book as there are too many variables to give consistent results. These factors can include obvious things such as the size and thickness of your ingredients or the amount of moisture in each item and even the humidity levels in the air.

As a guide to temperatures, a range of 40–75°C (104–167°F) will cover most ingredients in a slow, steady manner – the lower end for delicate leaves and flowers, the upper end for juicy fruits and roots. The trick is to regularly check your ingredients while they're drying so you capture them at their peak.

What to Grow

Growing your own ingredients can be an incredibly rewarding activity and, no matter where you live in the world, you'll have a decent range of plants to choose from. You don't need green fingers to be successful, but for those who are relatively new to gardening here are a few words of advice to get you up and running.

GETTING STARTED

When deciding what to grow, it's worth taking into consideration the natural habitat of each plant and choosing things that thrive in similar conditions to your garden. You can, of course, push the boundaries and introduce plants from other regions, but try to replicate their natural conditions as far as possible. For example, Mediterranean plants will likely want sunshine and good drainage; tropical plants will benefit from warmth all year round; and woodland plants will most likely thrive in the damper, shadier recesses of your garden.

Some folk go to great lengths to grow their favourite fruits, veg and flowers, but we prefer to adopt a much lazier attitude towards gardening: trial and error. If something refuses to grow without our full attention then we move on and give the space to something else instead. After all, we want time to enjoy relaxing in our gardens rather than spending an age weeding, pruning, feeding and nurturing.

Within this book you'll find a huge range of plants that will suit any style of garden – be it a rambling wildlife haven, a formal outdoor space or a collection of pots perched on a balcony. There's always room for a few tea-giving plants, be they trees, flowers, vegetables or herbs... and we've covered the lot.

There are three main ways to get new plants into your garden – sowing seeds, propagating them from an existing plant, or buying an established plant.

SOWING SEEDS

This is a cheap way of getting lots of plants into your garden, and the range of seeds at your local garden centre is almost certainly going to be bigger than their range of established plants.

Not everything grows well from seed, and it can take more time and effort than other methods, but watching a tiny seedling turn into a big, leafy crop is extremely rewarding. Seed sowing is most valuable for annuals – plants that are sown, grow, flower, fruit and die all within one year.

For seed-sowing beginners, we recommend flowers such as marigold and chamomile or some vegetables, with beetroot being a good option to start with.

You can spend a long time searching the internet and reading books on how to best grow your chosen seeds but, more often than not, the concise advice printed on the back of the seed packet is the best.

TAKING CUTTINGS OR DIVIDING PLANTS

If you want to multiply some of your favourite plants then taking cuttings or dividing them is a free way of achieving this. The methods won't work for everything, so do some research to find out if propagation is achievable for what you want to grow. A cutting is simply a snippet of plant growth that is allowed to develop new roots, either by potting it in soil or placing it first in water. Some herbs including mint, lavender and rosemary are easy to cultivate by this method, while fruit bushes such as blackcurrants can also be grown this way.

Dividing involves breaking an established plant up into smaller pieces. It is suitable for some varieties that spread out their root system as they grow and don't mind being dug up and chopped. Bee balm, mint, lemongrass and rhubarb can all be divided easily.

BUYING ESTABLISHED PLANTS

Of course, the easiest method to quickly fill a patch of garden or container is to buy an established plant. It will be more expensive than the other methods, but will provide you with instant results for minimum effort. If you're not too sure on how or when to plant your new purchases then make sure you buy them from a reputable garden centre or nursery and ask the staff for advice. You should also check that your plant looks healthy, with no yellowing of the leaves, and that it hasn't become pot-bound – a condition where the roots grow too large for the container and wrap around the inside of the pot. Plants that are in a poor condition in their pots are less likely to thrive when they are planted out.

WHAT WE GROW

Nick grows a lot of his tea-making plants in pots – mint, lemon verbena and bay all sit next to his kitchen door for quick access to a fresh cuppa. He also stuffs his flower borders with other wild tea ingredients, including lavender, hyssop, marigold, chamomile and fennel. Even some wild plants, notably yarrow and a self-seeded elderflower, have been allowed space in the garden. He also has a small greenhouse, which is ideal for sowing seeds early in the year and has room for a few fruit bushes and some wild strawberries, while a rampant sage plant threatens to smother the lot.

Rich is the proud keeper of an allotment which is home to his five prized apple trees, a tangled mass of raspberry canes and most of his wild tea ingredients. He grows produce in raised beds and has given one over entirely to tea ingredients, including chamomile, borage and marigold (some of which came from Nick's greenhouse). Having the extra space of an allotment also gives him the opportunity to experiment with some of the more unusual ingredients in this book. He has given one bed over to three brewing grains: barley, oats and wheat. Around the edges of his allotment, Rich has carefully nurtured and protected several wild plants including nettles, dandelions and a rambling rose.*

* *Some folk might consider these invasive weeds. Not us.*

Rules of Foraging

Many of the ingredients mentioned in this book can be grown in the garden, but for some you'll need to venture out beyond the gate and do a spot of foraging. Plant finding and identification is a skill that takes patience and a keen eye, but a few days spent out and about in the countryside with a decent plant identification book or phone app will set you on the right course. Better still, join a local nature group or enrol on a foraging course run by people in the know. Before long, you'll start to see hedgerows as giant tea caddies and be able to spot a berry-bearing elder from three fields away.

THE FIVE GOLDEN RULES OF FORAGING

Before heading out with swag bag in hand, there are a few essential rules that the aspiring hedgetarian must adhere to for safe and responsible foraging:

1. Mind Where You Pick

The laws governing foraging are quite indistinct, with grey areas aplenty. The UK's Countryside Act states that foraging on common land is acceptable as long as it is for personal use, but local by-laws may override this. In the US, laws vary state by state. Wandering over private property without permission is, of course, trespass and you should steer well clear of nature reserves, conservation areas and areas of scientific interest. Use common sense when foraging and, wherever possible, seek permission first.

2. Mind What You Are Picking

Some plants are lethal to ingest, and there are countless horror stories of foraging folk undergoing hospital treatment after gobbling a wrongly identified plant. You may also unwittingly tug up a protected plant species, so be 100% sure of your quarry.

3. Pick in Moderation

Don't descend on and decimate a plant like a plague of locusts – leave plenty left behind for the birds, insects and mammals to enjoy. It is, after all, their pantry you are raiding.

4. Wash Before Use

Insects, insecticides and pollution are not conducive to a nice cup of tea. Rid your plants of contamination – visible or otherwise – before using. Discard anything that looks rotten or pongs.

5. Avoid Low-Level Picking on Pathways

Plants that live beside public thoroughfares will be at the mercy of every passing pooch. Always forage higher than a dog can cock its leg.

FORAGING KIT CHECKLIST

Now that you know the golden rules of foraging, you need to make sure you have the right kit with you, so you can collect and store your bounty in the best way:

Containers and Bags

You'll need a decent bag to hold your swag – foraged fruits can get a bit sweaty in a plastic bag, especially when gathered under the glare of the midday sun. Your flimsy receptacle may also come to a premature end when confronted with a thorny bush. A hessian or canvas tote bag is a good, durable option, especially when combined with a selection of Tupperware tubs to separate your stash.

Tools

A folding pruning knife can be useful for helping to persuade reluctant plants to give up their bounty. Likewise, a pair of long-nosed pruners may come in handy when delving deep for fruits or flowers borne on thorny bushes (see Gorse, *page 40*)

Protection

Protection is key when foraging. Thornproof gloves are handy for preventing cuts and scratches, but may prove restrictive for nimble picking. In wintertime, a pair of fingerless gloves can provide cold weather protection while providing the necessary dexterity for your digits. A coat with capacious pockets will keep you warm and dry and also provide extra storage space for your foraged goods.

Proper Tea

The plants, flowers, berries and roots mentioned in this book all make excellent brews, but for some folk, there is only one proper tea — the drink made from the leaves of *Camellia sinensis*. If you're a 'proper' fan, you can learn about its origins, how to grow it yourself, and how to identify different varieties here.

THE TEA PLANT

CAMELLIA SINENSIS

The plant is thought to have originated in southwestern China (*sinensis* means 'from China') and was used to make drinks for medicinal purposes in the third century AD. Its popularity spread during the Tang dynasty (AD 618–705) into neighbouring Asian countries, reaching Europe sometime during the sixteenth century. Today, it's grown in around forty-five countries in a wide variety of climates, from tropical mountainous regions to the damp, weedy conditions of our allotment here in the South West of England.

As with wines and ciders, the conditions in which the tea plant grows affect the taste and aroma of the final brew. These conditions — commonly known as 'terroir' — include soil types, local weather conditions and altitude. The most profound effect on flavour, however, is the way the tea leaves are processed after picking. Depending on the style of tea desired, teamakers will either macerate, roll or tumble tea leaves to break down their cells before allowing them to oxidize (or 'go brown' to you and I). The longer the leaves are left to oxidize, the darker and richer the tea will be. Green and white teas forgo the oxidization process, which results in a lighter, fresher brew.

For a lowdown on the various styles available, flip over the page for our tea spotter's guide.

LEGENDARY TEA

According to Japanese legend, Bodhidharma, a fifth-century Buddhist monk, first created tea. Disgusted with himself for falling asleep while meditating, Bodhi sliced off his own eyelids and flung them to the ground. The first tea plant (complete with eyelid-shaped leaves) sprung from his discarded eyelids. Bodhi (in wide-eyed in amazement) plucked the leaves and brewed the very first cuppa.

1. GROW IT

It's possible to grow a tea plant from seed, but germination can be quite a hit or miss affair. For ease, we'd suggest grabbing young plants, which are readily available from specialist nurseries and many online garden retailers.

Tea plants like growing in ericaceous (acidic) soil with good drainage, ideally in a spot that affords partial shade and shelter from the wind. Top-dress your tea plants annually with shredded bark or well-rotted leaf mould and water well during the summer months.

Although *Camellia sinensis* is frost hardy, pot-grown specimens can be susceptible to root damage caused by cold weather. To prevent a premature end to your tea plantation aspirations, swaddle pots with Bubble Wrap or fleece in the winter.

2. PICK IT

Tea plants take two to three years to reach maturity and will grow broad, bushy and tall if left unpruned. To keep them manageable – and to aid easy picking – commercial tea plantations trim their bushes waist height and flat to create a 'plucking table'. A tea plant is ready to be plucked when new, bright green growth (called the flush) starts to appear. For the best cup of tea, pluck the first two newly emerged leaves (including the bud) from the branch with a pincer action using your finger and thumb.

3. PREPARE IT

For Black Tea:

Take your plucked leaves and bruise them using a pestle and mortar or similar. Spread out the bruised leaves in a single layer and allow them to air dry for a couple of days. Place the leaves on a baking tray in an oven for 20 minutes at 100°C (212°F) before storing in an airtight container.

For Green Tea:

Place your leaves into a colander and steam them over a pan of boiling water for around 2–3 minutes. When cool, roll the leaves into long sausage shapes, then leave to dry in a warm place until crispy. Store your leaves in an airtight container.

HOW TO TAKE A CUTTING

If you fancy increasing your tea plant collection for minimum cash outlay, try propagating a cutting, snipped from your plant in late summer.

Find a developing leaf that is growing on a green stem on your donor plant, and cut the stem diagonally with a sharp knife, a finger's width above the leaf joint and two to three fingers below.

Plunge the cutting into a small pot filled with a decent potting soil and keep somewhere warm but out of direct sunlight. Ensure the plant gets a light spray of water daily.

When your plant reaches a height of around 20–30 cm (8–12 in), you need to harden it off over the course of three weeks to prepare it for outdoor life. During the first week, leave your plant outdoors, covered with a fleece and bring indoors at night. For week two, leave it outside, minus the fleece, but bring indoors at night. In week three, leave it outside during the day and cover with fleece during the night.

A Tea-Spotter's Guide

Below we've listed the most popular types of tea made from *Camellia sinensis* to help you identify them with ease.

GREEN TEA

The most favoured tea style in Asia. *Camellia sinensis* leaves are plucked and heated – either by pan firing or steaming – to prevent the leaves from oxidizing. This process helps retain the tea's verdant colour and grassy, herbaceous flavours.

WHITE TEA

White tea is the result of a long, gentle process where leaves (and sometimes unopened buds) are left to wither for a couple of days before being baked at a low heat. The tea doesn't undergo any rolling or oxidization which gives it a light, delicate flavour. White tea gets its name from the tiny white hairs* that cover the tips.

OOLONG TEA

To produce oolong tea, mature leaves are withered in sunlight before being bruised to help release the flavours prior to undergoing a partial oxidization. Oolong tea is then either rolled into long leaves or formed into tadpole like shapes. The taste of oolong can range from a fruity sweetness to herbal and savoury.

BLACK TEA

The ubiquitous teabag tea widely favoured for its full-bodied flavour and high caffeine content. Leaves are picked and bruised before undergoing full oxidization, turning them black. Heat is then applied to stop the oxidization, and the tea is graded for quality.

* *Naming it 'hairy tea' would have been an altogether trickier product to market.*

YELLOW TEA

Yellow tea is a rare, fragrant beast, made from the young buds taken from tea plants grown in select areas of China. Leaves are steamed so they oxidize slowly, which results in a straw-coloured brew with a smooth, mellow taste.

PU'ER TEA

This tea is the leafy equivalent of an aged whisky. It's made from the large-leafed subspecies *Camellia sinensis* var. *assamica*, grown in Yunnan Province, southwestern China, which is fermented with a special bacterium then pressed into cake shapes and left to age. Because the tea is in a constant state of flux, no two teas will taste the same.

MATCHA TEA

Tea destined to be turned into matcha is shade-grown for three to four weeks before harvest which stimulates chlorophyll production, hence the tea's bright green hue. In the matcha-making process, leaves' veins and stems are painstakingly removed before being ground into a fine powder, which results in a concentrated, caffeine-packed brew.

FLAVOURED TEA

Adding flavouring was once used as a way of disguising poor quality black teas – much like those supermarket cheeses that come in daft flavours (and quite a few fruit-flavoured ciders, for that matter). Perhaps the most popular example is Earl Grey, which is flavoured with bergamot oil. Lapsang souchong gets its smoky flavour by drying leaves over pinewood fires.

Milks

There was a time, in our youth, when milk was simply defined by the amount of cream it contained. But in these more health- and environmentally-conscious times, not only is there a greater choice of dairy milk products to be had, but there's a bandwagon loaded with dairy-free milk alternatives that is rolling to a supermarket near you.

While many of the drinks made from nuts, grains and seeds bear only a passing resemblance to the taste of anything a cow might produce, plenty of them are perfectly effective in a cup of tea, providing some of the whitening, texture-smoothing and flavour-softening that would traditionally be performed by milk.

If you're new to plant-based milk alternatives then the trick is to try a few different types and find the one that best suits your preferred drinks. For example, we reckon almond milk works a treat in a cup of chai; we count on coconut for the most terrific turmeric latté; but when it comes to black tea, oat milk wins out.

Another great thing about milk alternatives is that you can even make some of them yourself, which (unless you're in charge of a dairy herd) is not something you can say about milk produced by a cow.

OAT MILK

For this recipe you'll need to get hold of some rolled oats. You can invest in an elaborate rolling machine that will mill and roll your own, home-grown oats (see *page 82*), but to be honest it's far easier to source some from the shops.

Makes: 4 cups
1 cup rolled oats
4 cups water
A pinch of salt
½ tsp vanilla extract and 1–2 tsp honey or maple syrup
   (optional, see right)

1 Pour your oats into a large bowl and cover with water, then set aside and leave to soak for 15–20 minutes.

2 Pour the soggy oats into a sieve, rinse under a cold tap, then transfer to a food processor.

3 Add the water and salt, and the vanilla extract, honey or maple syrup (if using), then blend on full power for 1–2 minutes.

4 Finally, strain the oaty mixture through a sieve and chill before serving.

HAZELNUT MILK

The method given here for hazelnut milk can be applied to pretty much any kind of nut-based milk, but as hazelnuts are easily foraged near us, it's them we turn to for our wild and milky drinks. Goes well with coffee, too.

Makes: 3 cups
1 cup shelled, raw hazelnuts
3 cups water
½ tsp vanilla extract and 1–2 tsp honey
   or maple syrup (optional, see below)

1 First you need to soak the nuts by putting them in a bowl and covering them with water. Leave them in the fridge overnight (or for around 8 hours).

2 After soaking, pour off the liquid and give your nuts a good rinse in cold water.*

3 Put the nuts into a blender with the water and blast until they have seemingly disappeared.

4 This liquid now needs straining. You can actually buy specialist 'nut milk bags', but a traditional fine straining cloth, such as muslin, will work just as effectively. Make sure you give your crushed nuts as hard a squeeze as you can muster to extract every last drop of goodness. Add the vanilla extract, honey or maple syrup now (if using).

5 Store the liquid in a sealed bottle or jar and keep it in the fridge, where it will last for two days. The liquid separates if left alone, so make sure you shake your milky nut juice before each use.

OPTIONAL FLAVOUR ENHANCERS

Although we find these simple nut and oat milk recipes perfectly acceptable for cups of tea, some people prefer extra flavour and sweetness to make them more dairy-like when poured onto their morning muesli. If this sounds like you then try whisking in ½ tsp of vanilla extract and 1–2 tsp of honey or maple syrup.

* Some folk suggest peeling off the hazelnut's dark outer layer at this stage but we don't think this is necessary. If you disagree and insist on a whiter milk then turn to page 171 for nut-blanching instructions.

Top 40 Ingredients

Whether grown, foraged or bought,
these are our favourite choices for
brewing a wild tea.

Blackberry

(*Rubus fruticosus*)

We'd wager that most folks' first foray into foraging is blackberry picking with their parents. We can still remember the excitement of picking these juicy jewels – for every berry nabbed, you'd pop at least five in your mouth. Blackberry bushes grow in abundance and you can brew both the berries and leaves, so load up in springtime when the fresh leaves start to appear, then in late summer enjoy the bountiful berry bonus.

FORAGE IT

Search for blackberry bushes in hedges, lanes and across urban wasteland. According to folklore, the berries shouldn't be picked after Michaelmas (29 September) as the Devil will either spit on them, pee on them, fondle them or generally manhandle them, depending on the stories that abound in your region. However, the spoiling of blackberry crops at this time is probably down to the cooler, damper weather rather than demonic intervention. Store picked berries in a cool dry place (they should last for a couple of days) or just freeze them for later. Pick the leaves and tips when they are young and fresh, before they develop tough spines on their undersides.

GROW IT

To all intents and purposes there doesn't seem much point in cultivating your own blackberry bushes given their abundance in the countryside, but there are a few varieties available to grow in a garden or allotment that are well worth considering. 'Loch Ness' will offer you wild-tasting fruit on a thornless plant, while the fruit of the 'Karaka Black' grow large and flavoursome. For those after a plant that can live happily in a container, consider the compact but tasty 'Loch Tay'.

The majority of blackberry varieties will grow fruit on one-year old canes, so prune to the base after harvesting the berries and tie or support any newly emerging canes the following spring.

BREW THE LEAVES

Blackberry leaves make fantastic tea and can be treated in much the same way as you would the leaves of *Camellia sinensis*. You can brew with fresh leaves but the best way of making blackberry leaf tea is to bruise the young leaves before allowing them to dry naturally so that they oxidize. The longer you leave them, the more intense flavour they will release. To make your cuppa, crumble them up and steep 2–3 tsp in hot water for 5–10 minutes.

DID YOU KNOW?

During the American Civil War, blackberry tea was drunk by both Confederate and Union troops in an attempt to cure the rampant dysentery that plagued both sides. Ceasefires were often called so that soldiers could go out and forage for fruits to help stem the tide.

BREW THE BERRIES

Mash up a handful of blackberries,* push the resulting mush through a sieve, and leave the syrup that is released to rest for a couple of hours on a warm windowsill to steep. Pour the mixture into a mug and top up with hot water. Enjoy.

For a nice icy summertime treat, head on over to *page 172* and try our blinding Blackberry Frappé recipe.

HEALTH BENEFITS

Blackberries pack plenty of fibre and contain decent amounts of vitamin C and vitamin K (vitamins that are commonly found in green leaves), which are an essential aid to the blood-clotting process that heals wounds. Blackberry leaf tea is also said to be an effective cure for acute diarrhoea.

BLEND IT

Delve further into the hedgerow and try mixing the berry juice with its countryside cousin elderberry for a dark and fruity brew. Use the leaves instead of green tea in healthy, caffeine-free blends.

* Blackberries also bring an autumnal, deep red hue to infusions that looks instantly healthy. (The ivy in the picture above is purely for photogenic purposes – its poisonous leaves are most definitely not healthy.)

Blackcurrant

(Ribes nigrum)

The blackcurrant is one of the most versatile home-grown ingredients in the tea maker's caddy – both its fruit and leaves are suitable for brewing. The leaves are full of tannin that gives a robustness similar to black tea. Used on its own, as a double act or blended with other ingredients, blackcurrant rewards the drinker with a healthy tea full of tart curranty goodness.

GROW IT

Blackcurrants are one of the easiest soft fruit bushes to grow and are even suitable for containers. They're sold as 'bare root stock' (the sticks have exposed roots) or in pots, and should be planted out during their dormant period between November and March. Before planting, give the roots a good soaking, then dig a large hole (around twice the diameter and depth of the roots when spread out), half fill with compost or manure, sink in the sticks and fill with more compost. The dormant period is also the time to prune your currant bushes. As the fruit is more bountiful on younger branches, it's the old ones that should be removed, along with any that are weak or damaged.

There are a few varieties of blackcurrant to choose from – we've always enjoyed good results from one called 'Ben Lomond.'

BERRY HYBRIDS

Botanists like to experiment with berries, including blackcurrants, and have come up with a number of hybrids. Here are five curranty couplings that can give your teas a twist.

Jostaberry

This cross between a blackcurrant and a gooseberry produces dark berries that start out dominated by the tart flavour of a gooseberry before taking on more of a blackcurrant flavour as they mature.

Loganberry, Tayberry and Tummelberry

Three different fruits, each the result of crossing blackberries with raspberries, and all coming in various shades of red.

Boysenberry

This sees the blackberry crossed again with one of its own offspring, the loganberry, to produce a sweeter kind of blackberry.

Silvanberry

An Australian creation, this is a cross between a boysenberry and a marionberry (a blackberry cultivar). It's essentially a blackberry.

Chuckleberry

This daftly named fruit is a mongrel of the berry world, being a cross between a redcurrant, gooseberry and jostaberry (see above). It grows like a blackcurrant and is a high-yielding plant.

BREW THE BERRIES

The berries make an excellent rich and fruity tea with a distinctive tartness. To make, crush around 15 fresh berries by pressing them against the inside of a mug with a teaspoon (or for those who like getting messy with purple stains, a pinch between finger and thumb also works) before adding enough boiling water to fill the mug to the top. Allow the berries to steep for as long as possible for maximum flavour. You can also use dried or frozen fruits.

BREW THE LEAVES

The leaves share some of the flavours of the fruit, along with a fresh 'greenness', and are packed with tannin which will give your tea a bite. You'll need around 10 mid-sized fresh leaves per cup. Give them a scrunch before adding the boiling water and remove after 4–5 minutes to prevent the tannins from taking over. They also work extremely well dried, with 1–2 tsp being sufficient for a brew.

HEALTH BENEFITS

Blackcurrants are packed full of vitamin C, making the tea one of the healthiest you can brew. They have also been referred to as 'gout berries', due to their ability to regulate the uric acid levels in the body that are responsible for gout and joint pains.

BLEND IT

The berries combine well with other fruits and experimenters can have fun introducing them to a few fragrant flowers such as rose or lavender. The leaves are great at adding a depth of flavour and bite to other ingredients – try a pinch in a mug of mint tea to give it a curranty punch.

DID YOU KNOW?

It has been illegal to grow blackcurrants in many American states since the early twentieth century, as the plants were held responsible for transmitting the disease white pine blister rust which damages native forests.

Raspberry

(Rubus idaeus)

This beloved bringer of small ruddy fruits grows prolifically on our allotment, despite occupying the site of our longest running battle with weeds. Due to a slipshod mulching policy, summertime sees the raspberry patch overrun with bindweed – a plant-strangling perennial whose sole aim seems to be to tug down the berry-bearing canes and spoil our crop. Untangling the raspberries is a tedious but necessary task, for our bushes provide us with both fruit for jams and puddings and with terrific tannic leaves that are perfect for turning into tea.

GROW IT

Raspberries favour rich, well-drained, slightly acidic soil, preferably in a nice, sunny spot that is sheltered from strong winds. Plant them out between September and March while they are dormant. Dig some well-rotted manure into your chosen planting site and plant in rows, with each cane around 0.6 m (2 ft) apart. There are two types of raspberry: summer fruiting and autumn fruiting. Summer fruiting plants are usually trained up a frame or post and wire support, but autumn fruiting raspberries can be left to their own devices. These are also the best bet for growing in a patio-based container.

To keep your plants healthy and productive, pruning is essential. If you have autumn-fruiting canes, chop down the lot in winter. Summer-fruiting canes need a little more care, so make sure you cut down the canes after they have fruited (the woody ones), but leave the newer, greener canes so that they can produce fruit the following season. If you plan to grow both types, it's a good idea to plant them apart. The spreading nature of the runners means that the two varieties will soon intermingle if planted too close, causing extreme pruning confusion.

Your raspberry patch will benefit from a drop of fertilizer in early spring. Mulching the base with well rotted manure will also help keep pesky weeds at bay. If you treat them well, your raspberries will reward you with ten or more years of fruity pleasure.

BREW IT

To make the best raspberry leaf tea, pluck the youngest leaves from the stems and allow them to dry. Use 1–2 tsp per cup and leave to infuse in a cup full of boiling water for 5–10 minutes. For added fruitiness, try drying out a few raspberry fruits (best done in a dehydrator) and drop them into your cup along with the leafy mix.

DID YOU KNOW?

Raspberries hail from the same genus (*Rubus*) and family (Rosaceae) as the blackberry, but what distinguishes the two is the stem (or torus). When you pick a blackberry, the stem stays with the fruit, while the raspberry leaves its stem behind, clinging to the plant.

HEALTH BENEFITS

Raspberry leaf tea is often taken by pregnant women as it is believed to tone the uterus in preparation for the rigors of labour. In contrast, raspberry fruit tea tends to be taken purely for pleasure, but the fruits do contain decent amounts of anthocyanins which are linked to a wide variety of health claims, including cancer prevention and the slowing of dementia symptoms.

BLEND IT

Try combining raspberry leaves with blackberry leaves, adding a twist of lemon for good measure. Raspberry and peppermint also make a tasty pairing, and the fruits make a tart addition to both sun teas and fruit teas.

Spruce and Pine

(Picea and Pinus)

As spring turns to summer, the bright green new growth of spruce and pine tips emerge from their papery cases. They possess the freshest, cleanest essence of the forest, which produces one of the best-smelling teas around. Those tips are also packed with vitamin C, adding a healthy boost to its olfactory excellence.

FORAGE IT

Spruce (*Picea*) and pine (*Pinus*) tips first appear in late spring – soft, feathery and almost glowing with vibrant green. The varieties differ in looks and flavour, so hunt around to decide on your favourite. Also, do check what you're picking as similar-looking plants (notably yew) are poisonous. The tips pinch off easily, but don't get carried away by taking too many from one tree as you'll deprive it of the chance to fully grow.

GROW IT

If you fancy sticking a spruce or pine tree in the garden, then why not wait until December and get a pot-grown Christmas tree (first checking with the grower that it hasn't been treated with chemicals if you're going to consume any of it). You should be able to nurse it through to spring with a bit of care. The popular Norway spruce is an excellent choice for tea-making.

BREW IT

A small handful of tips (around 15 average-sized tips) steeped in boiled water is enough for a cup of fresh tea, which is so popular in Sweden that it has its own name: *tallstrunt*. Tips are freezable and they also dry well, with 1 large tsp being sufficient for a brew. Older needles can be used to make tea, but they start to become more bitter and take on astringent flavours reminiscent of floor cleaning products, which is clearly not ideal.

HEALTH BENEFITS

Spruce and pine tips are so full of vitamin C that historically they were packed onto ocean-going vessels to help prevent scurvy among the crew. These days, people use them to treat a common cold. However, these are also ingredients with heavy cautions attached and should not be taken in large doses or by anyone who is pregnant or breastfeeding.

BLEND IT

The fresh lemony flavours of spruce and pine make them an interesting alternative to other lemon-tasting ingredients like lemon verbena and lemongrass. They also make a good addition to a simple cup of green tea.

DID YOU KNOW?

Spruce and pine get their lemon flavours from limonene, one of several chemical compounds known as terpenes that are also found in citrus fruits. Pinene is another terpene present and is responsible for those piney flavours. Both compounds are used in cleaning products.

Hops

(Humulus lupulus)

Hops are best known for their use in beer, with cultivated varieties producing a wide range of flavours, including citrus fruit, currant and pine, and also imparting that all-important bitterness. These attributes contribute to an excellent, soothing cup of tea. It's the flowers (or cones) of the hop plant that contain the essential flavouring oils and they also make an attractive addition to the garden – particularly if, like us, you've got an untidy brewing shed for the plants to ramble over and hide.

FORAGE IT

You'll often find wild hops rambling through hedges. The plants are most easily spotted when the hop cones start to form on the vines, which happens from midsummer onwards. Hops need to be picked at their prime for best results – the boxout (right) tells you all you need to know.

GROW IT

Although you can grow hops from seed, by far the best option is growing them from bare root stalks called rhizomes. Plant them in deep, well-drained soil in early spring. Hops grown· commercially are typically trained to grow up tall trellises, which can reach heights of 7.6 m (25 ft). For a smaller, more manageable hop variety, try 'Prima Donna', which should top out at around 2.4 m (8 ft) but still provide plenty of hop cones for your brewing endeavours.

WHEN TO PICK YOUR HOPS

Most hops in the UK are ready to harvest towards the end of August and through September. As the hops swell, they take on a vibrant, fresh green colour.

When ready, the vividness begins to fade and you'll start to see some browning around the edges. Hops that are ready will feel dry and papery – gently rub them between finger and thumb and the petals are more likely to break off and your digits will feel sticky and oily.

Break up a cone and at the base of the petals you'll see the powdery yellow lupulin dotted around. This contains the all-important hop acids and essential oils that impart the flavour.

If you're still unsure then wait a little longer – for brewing purposes, an overripe hop is better than an underripe hop.

BREW IT

Most brewers of beer will create a 'tea' to help them predict the way a finished beer will taste (see *page 150*) and you can use the same method to produce a hot tasty beverage. We'd recommend using hops that are low in alpha acids (which determine the bitterness of the hop) such as 'Kent Goldings' or 'Hallertau', as those with high alphas will make your tea unpleasantly bitter.

To brew a hot hoppy cuppa, simply toss 4–5 fresh cones into a cup of boiling water and leave to infuse for 5–10 minutes before straining and serving.

HEALTH BENEFITS

The hop is a plant heralded for its sedative properties and when steeped to make tea, you'll reap all of its snooze-giving goodness. Hops can also help with restlessness and irritability, and we can reliably confirm that these conditions are indeed relieved by a swift visit to a pub.

BLEND IT

Try mixing dried hops with nettles for an earthy, green-tinted brew. The zesty essence of lemon balm or lemon verbena also works well when combined (see *page 127*). Hops can also be used with other calm-inducing ingredients, such as those found in Sue's Hop to Bed Tea (see *page 126*).

DID YOU KNOW?

The hops' habit of wrapping itself around surrounding vegetation led the Romans to believe that it could strangle and kill other plants. It was given the predatory name of 'little wolf', which is a translation of the Latin genus name *Lupulus*.

Lime Flower

(*Tilia cordata*)

One of the most overlooked summer fragrances belongs to the lime (or linden) tree* – perhaps because the blossom is mostly above nose height. But gather a handful of the delicate flowers, breathe in their aroma, and you will be rewarded with a wonderful, sweet perfume of ripe melon and honey. The resulting tea is particularly popular in France, where it's known as *tilleul* and keeps Parisians in a calm, relaxed state of mind after a day stuck on the Boulevard Périphérique.

FORAGE IT

Lime trees are often quite old,** so look around established parks or country estates to find them. The flowers speckle the trees in summer, as the days reach their maximum length, and are often covered with bees – its pollen is much appreciated by bee-keepers for the tasty honey it produces. You should be able to gather enough blossoms at head height, but to maximize your picking potential a chair or ladder will come in handy.

BREW IT

The leaves and even the bark of the lime tree can be used to make a variety of potions, but it's the flowers that make the best tea. You can use them fresh, but they are generally better when dried. The honey aroma remains after brewing and the flavour is clean and light, making a tea that is both calming and refreshing. Steep 1–2 tsp for 5–10 minutes. Sweet-toothed drinkers looking for extra comfort can stir in a teaspoon of honey.

HEALTH BENEFITS

Some people believe that lime flowers will ease colds and headaches as well as regenerate the skin, but lime flower tea is most often used to bring a sense of calm to the drinker, making it a good beverage during anxious moments or before heading off to bed (see *page 126*).

BLEND IT

Lime flower is most commonly blended with other sleep-inducing ingredients such as chamomile and lavender.

DID YOU KNOW?

Marcel Proust, in his novel *In Search of Lost Time*, describes how a petite madeleine dipped in lime flower tea sets off a childhood memory and has led to the phrase 'Proust's madeleine' being used as an expression for such memory triggers.

---

* *No relation to the citrus lime fruit, our tea-making blossom comes from the* Tilia *genus of trees.*

** *Westonbirt, The National Arboretum, in Gloucestershire, England, has a coppiced lime tree which is believed to be around 2,000 years old.*

Gorse

(Ulex europaeus)

Gorse (also known as whin or furze) is a large, prickly member of the pea family, prized by foragers for its egg-yolk yellow flowers which can impart a distinctive coconut flavour to drinks and syrups. Its heady scent becomes more pungent in the heat of the sun, while the popping sounds of the seed heads may well punctuate a summer stroll through heathland and scrub. Gorse produces flowers all year round, so with a bit of searching (and providing you like the distinctive flavour that the flowers impart) your tea mug need never run dry.

FORAGE IT

With its bright yellow flower heads contrasting against the dark foliage, a gorse in bloom is easy to spot. It flourishes in poor soil conditions and is a common sight on heathland, roadsides, cliffs and fields. Foraging for gorse flowers can be a sweary business thanks to the plants fearsome thorns. We suggest using a pair of long-nosed scissors, snipping the blooms directly into your chosen receptacle.

GROW IT

Gorse is a great choice if you are looking to create an impenetrable barrier hedge to help keep out livestock* and intruders. You can grow gorse from seed, gathered on your foraging excursions. Soak seeds in water for 24 hours, then sow into trays, preferably under glass. Propagation can be a bit erratic, so for a more reliable option, buy a young plant from your local nursery or garden centre. Keep your newly planted gorse weed-free until the roots establish and give it a good pruning in early spring.

BREW IT

To make a tasty cup of tea, take 1 tsp of gorse flowers, add them to a cup of boiling water and let them steep for 10 minutes before straining. Alternatively, let your brew cool and add ice and a slice of lemon for a subtle summertime sipper.

HEALTH BENEFITS

When scarlet fever was rife, children suffering from the disease were often given an infusion of the flowers to ease symptoms. And while we wouldn't necessarily endorse it as a toothpaste substitute, chewing a mouthful of gorse blossoms mixed with honey makes for a half-decent mouth cleanser after a night on the beer.

BLEND IT

Try creating a Thai-inspired tea by blending your gorse flowers with a 2 cm (¾ in) piece of lemongrass and ½ tsp of ginger.

DID YOU KNOW?

The gorse flower was once used as a soap substitute by combining it with clay. Presumably care would have been taken to remove the thorns first.

* *Disclaimer: During the eighteenth and nineteenth centuries, gorse was widely used as animal fodder, so you may well attract more hooved beasts than you repel.*

Hawthorn

(Crataegus monogyna)

The hawthorn (or May tree) has long been a forager's favourite. The young, emerging leaves* and berries can be eaten directly from the bush and have earned the nickname 'bread and cheese' (despite tasting of neither bread nor cheese). Its nutty-flavoured foliage is a tasty addition to salads, but the hawthorn excels when it comes to hot, steamy beverages. Leaves, flowers, berries – you can brew the lot.

FORAGE IT

Like many plants destined for the teapot, the young leaves are the most flavoursome. The same applies to the flowers, which you should pick soon after they emerge. You'll have to wait a bit longer for the berries to arrive, but be patient – underripe fruits will produce weak, tasteless tea, so ideally you'll want to hold back until they are nice and plump. To test whether your berries are ready for the pot, give them a gentle squeeze – if the fleshy parcel gives a little, you are good to go.

BREW THE FLOWERS AND LEAVES

Dunk a fresh sprig (leaves and flowers) into a cup of boiling water and leave it to infuse for 5–10 minutes for a delicately- flavoured, green-hued brew. For a more intense hit, dry the leaves

DID YOU KNOW?

The hawthorn is a plant shrouded in superstition. In folklore, it is believed to be a harbinger of death, not least because the pungent pong of the hawthorn flower reportedly smells like rotting flesh. In the poem 'Whitsun', Sylvia Plath recalls picnicking among the 'death stench of hawthorn'. We'd argue that our tea smells a tad more fragrant.

first, then roughly chop them up and use 1–2 tsp per cup.

BREW THE BERRIES

Wash your berry bounty, then slice them up before drying, ideally in a dehydrator. Add 2 tsp per cup, pour on freshly boiled water and leave to infuse for 10 minutes for a pleasant, slightly tannic, orange-hued brew.

HEALTH BENEFITS

Hawthorns have been used for centuries to lower blood pressure and improve circulation, and the fruit is a key player in traditional Chinese medicine. Caution is advised though – gobbling down vast quantities may have an adverse effect on the heart and cause palpitations. That said, you should be fine sipping a few cups of tea.

BLEND IT

Try blending the berries with hawthorn's hedgerow pal the rosehip for a vitamin C-packed, health-giving brew.

* Older leaves, like stale bread and cheese, are inedible.

Elder

(*Sambucus nigra*)

Old countryside wisdom states that an English summer starts with the arrival of elderflowers and ends when the berries are ripe. We've endured a few lousy summers that have started in mid-August and ended in torrential downpours a couple of weeks later, but we get the general idea. Elderflowers are, of course, synonymous with the making of elderflower champagne – everyone's favourite hedgerow booze. If you can resist using all of your gathered stash for this fizzy treat, try setting some aside for a floral-forward cuppa. In late August, return to the elder and plunder its berries for pummelling into dark and funky brews.

FORAGE IT

If possible, collect your elderflowers before noon, because as soon as the midday sun starts to heat up the flowers, they start to give off a heady smell not dissimilar to cat pee. Give them a good shake and wash them well, as you'll most likely find a menagerie of insects lurking among the flowers, the likes of which are not necessarily conducive to a nice brew. Pick the berries when they ripen to a deep purple hue in late summer. Be aware that the berries (and leaves, stems, shoots and roots) are toxic until cooked, so don't be tempted to have a nibble while out picking.

GROW IT

You shouldn't have much trouble sourcing elderberries and flowers in the wild, but if you fancy growing an elder in your garden we would suggest trying 'Black Lace'. It's a dark-leaved, pink-flowering, handsome bush that will take to most soil conditions. Elder also grows easily from cuttings – simply thrust a stick into soil and there's a good chance it will take root.

BREW THE FLOWERS

Put 3 tsp dried elderflowers in a cup and fill up with boiling water. Let it steep for 5–10 minutes. Strain and sweeten with honey to taste.

BREW THE BERRIES

Dried berries make a decent cup of tea, but using fresh berries is a tad more involving. A tea brewed from elderberries alone can be pretty tangy, so it pays to add a few spices to make it into a chai. Grab a fistful of fresh elderberries, pound them into a paste, then place this in a saucepan. Add 2 cardamom pods, ½ a cinnamon stick, 1 tsp of freshly grated ginger and 300 ml (10 fl oz) of water. Bring to a boil and simmer for 10 minutes. Strain into a mug and enjoy.

DID YOU KNOW?

It is thought that flies are repelled by the scent of elder leaves, so elder bushes were often planted outside fly-frequented buildings such as latrines, farm buildings and slaughterhouses.

HEALTH BENEFITS

Elderflowers are thought to have antiseptic and anti-inflammatory properties and are often used in traditional medicine to help treat sinusitis and joint pains. Elderberries are a strong antioxidant and pack plenty of fibre.

BLEND IT

A brew made from elderflowers requires subtle flavour combinations – try adding raspberry leaves or rose petals; but elderflowers are arguably at their best in a summery iced tea (see *page 158*). The bold berries work well with other dark hedgerow fruits and the addition of spices.

Meadowsweet

(Filipendula ulmaria)

You'll find this wispy-haired member of the rose family growing in hedgerows, on cliff tops and in damp meadows. The name meadowsweet is derived from the Anglo-Saxon word *medesweete* as the plant was once used in the making of mead, – the heady, honey-based booze renowned for bestowing fearful hangovers on the inexperienced imbiber. Ironically, the plant contains salicin, a precursor to the drug aspirin, making meadowsweet both a cause and a cure for a banging head. Feeling a bit fragile? A cup of meadowsweet tea might be just the tonic.

FORAGE IT

Meadowsweet is an easy one to spot, thanks to the white frothy blooms billowing forth from tall reddish stems. Its sweet, almond-like scent is also a strong giveaway, which becomes more intense and pronounced after picking – you'll certainly notice a pleasing pong as the flowers sit drying on your kitchen window.

GROW IT

Although meadowsweet prefers growing wild and free, it can be persuaded to inhabit a garden setting. It prefers full sun but will also flourish in semi-shade. Plant it in rich, moist soil if you can, mulch it with well-rotted manure and cut back after flowering.

BREW IT

Meadowsweet tea is taken more for its perceived health benefits than for taste, but we think there's a certain understated charm to its subtle, straw-like flavour. Add 1 tsp of dried flowers to a cup of boiling water, leave to infuse for 10 minutes then strain before drinking.

HEALTH BENEFITS

Along with helping to stem the misery of a throbbing head, meadowsweet has traditionally been used as a digestive aid. The plant is also used as a cure for diarrhoea and in the treatment of inflammatory diseases. It also contains salicylic acid, which is used in the production of aspirin, so be extra careful when drinking it and only do so in moderation – it should not be consumed during pregnancy and by anyone with an aspirin allergy. Folks who suffer from asthma should also give this plant a wide berth.

BLEND IT

Owing to its delicate nature, meadowsweet is not often used in blended brews but you can try it in our Coastal Cuppa on *page 123*.

DID YOU KNOW?

Meadowsweet was used extensively in the Middle Ages as a strewing herb. Strewing herbs were scattered onto floors so that they would release a perfumed scent when crushed underfoot and mask unpleasant odours. In those days of open sewers, plagues and a slack approach to personal hygiene, there would have been many odours to mask.

Hibiscus

(*Hibiscus sabdariffa*)

There are hundreds of species of hibiscus,* which belongs to the mallow family, but it's Roselle (sometimes known as Red Sorell) that is widely cultivated for culinary use. Its tart, fruity flavours have been put to good use in numerous drinks, jams, sauces, syrups and even pickles where it quickly imparts its strong flavour and vivid red colour to whatever it meets. A colourful essential for your tea caddy.

GROW IT

If you fancy growing your own from seed, you will need to make small incisions into the hard coating and soak the seeds in warm water for 2 hours prior to planting. The plants then need careful nurturing, particularly in a cold and wet climate like ours, and will bloom as summer fades to autumn. This is all slightly too much bother for us,** but thankfully dried hibiscus is readily available.

BREW IT

It's actually the red calyces of hibiscus that are used for beverages (the bits that surround the bud before flowering – they're green on most plants such as roses) and their fiddly removal is another reason to go down the shop-bought route. To make a tea simply steep 1 tsp of dried calyces in hot water for 5 minutes and you'll be rewarded with a bright red liquid that has a tart, fruity flavour.

HEALTH BENEFITS

There has been recent research into hibiscus tea to determine if it can help lower blood pressure and cholesterol. Its effect on the former has shown more promising results thus far (but our natural scepticism means we'll wait for more convincing evidence).

BLEND IT

Hibiscus has such a fruity flavour that many commercial tea blends claiming to be made with fruit actually have hibiscus as their main ingredient. For home blending it's great for adding to dried fruits and berries, particularly if you want to capitalize on its red colour. It also works well in iced teas (see *page 149*) and gives a punchy flavour to floral blends.

---

* Some folk claim all varieties are edible, but we can't find evidence that they've all been tested. Stick to Hibiscus sabdariffa.

** We once successfully germinated some seeds but the young plants perished while on holiday.

Yarrow

(Achillea millefolium)

We think yarrow is one of the most underappreciated wild plants around. Its masses of small white (and occasionally pink-tinged) flowers look as good in gardens as they do in hedgerows, while its wispy, furry leaves make a superb cup of tea. Despite this, it doesn't seem to have caught on outside of the foraging fraternity, so head out into the fields and brew a cup – the yarrow appreciation club starts here.

FORAGE IT

Yarrow is common throughout Europe, Asia and North America, growing on roadside verges, meadows, river banks and just about anywhere else it's allowed to settle. It flowers from June to September and novice foragers should be careful to avoid confusion with similar looking white-flowering plants, particularly the deadly hemlock, so study its feathery leaves to help you to identify it correctly.

GROW IT

Other achillea cultivars are popular with gardeners, but yarrow is seen more as a weed. We think this harsh, finding it the most naturally attractive of the family, and have gladly allowed it into our gardens (although its vast armies of tiny seeds do have a habit of invading lawns). Insects love its flat-topped floral landing pads, which makes it an even more welcome member of our borders.

BREW IT

The leaves have a slight bitterness, which makes them a brilliant addition to beers (but as with tea you'll struggle to find it featured in many commercial brews). They're best used fresh for tea, giving a flavour not too dissimilar to green tea – full of green vitality with an added earthiness. Flavour intensity can fluctuate, but around 3–5 fresh leaves, depending on size, should be sufficient when steeped in a cup of hot water, or 1 tsp of dried leaves and flowers.

HEALTH BENEFITS

There is a huge list of mostly unsubstantiated health benefits attributed to yarrow – from curing fevers and healing wounds to treating haemorrhoids and skin conditions – but it should be used in moderation as it can cause rashes in some cases and is toxic to cats, dogs and horses.

BLEND IT

As with green tea it goes very well with lemon or mint.

DID YOU KNOW?

According to Greek mythology, Achilles used yarrow to heal his soldiers' wounds. The latin name *Achillea millefolium* is derived from the Greek words *achilleios*, which means 'herb of Achilles', and *myriophyllon*, which translates as 'countless leaves'.

Mint

(Mentha)

If you grow one wild tea, make it mint. The herb is one of the easiest to grow and produces a constant supply of leaves from spring through to mid-autumn which can be used on their own or in a huge range of tea blends. Get yourself a container, stick it in the garden or on the windowsill, and treat yourself to a ready supply of instant refreshment.

GROW IT

Mint has a habit of rapidly spreading its roots, so confine it to pots if you don't want it to take over your garden. The plants die back over winter and eagerly emerge as the spring warmth builds, increasing their coverage a little further each year. Mint is also easy to cultivate from cuttings: simply snip off a finger-length tip of stem just below a pair of leaves, remove the lower leaves and stick the stem in a glass, filling it with water to below the leaves. Before long, roots will emerge and you can pot it up in compost. If you find a plant you like then it's a great way to share the minty goodness with your friends.

BREW IT

Around 10 fresh leaves is sufficient for a cup, but you can pack as much of a minty punch as you like by adding more. Scrunch leaves before infusing with hot water to help release the flavour. Mint is also excellent dried with 1 tsp being enough for a mug.

HEALTH BENEFITS

Besides freshening breath (see Morning After the Night before Tea, *page 126*) mint's main medical claims relate to the stomach: it can aid digestion and soothe pains, particularly when overeating is responsible (see *page 126*).

BLEND IT

Although mint can be a dominant flavour, it works well with most things, so put on your experimental hat and dream up some ingenious new combinations. For the classic Moroccan Mint Tea see *page 137*.

FIVE MINT VARIETIES

Wander around a well-stocked garden centre and you're likely to find a wide range of mints, many claiming to have tastes similar to other foods (such as pineapple mint, chocolate mint or banana mint). For tea makers, here are five mints we think it's worth getting to know:

Spearmint

Also known as common mint, garden mint, mackerel mint and sage of Bethlehem, this is the classic upright, bushy mint with vivid green, tooth-edged leaves and sweet menthol flavours that make it great for all culinary uses, including teas.

Peppermint

A hybrid of spearmint and water mint, this herb is bolstered with extra menthol (40% compared to less than 1% in spearmint). Besides the increased minty flavour, it's also spicier and

is often the preferred choice in commercially produced dried teas.

Moroccan mint

Moroccan mint is a type of spearmint with more compact leaves. Obviously it's a good choice for Moroccan mint tea.

Apple mint

One of our favourite mints for the garden, this variety grows tall, has light green fluffy leaves and is also known as tickle mint. It has a deliciously sweet and fruity minty flavour.

Ginger mint

Also known as Scotch mint, this is a cross between spearmint and corn mint. It's often seen showing off stripes on its leaves and has a subtle spicy warmth to its flavour.

Dandelion

(Taraxacum officinale)

For us, the dandelion is a welcome sight in spring, with its showy yellow flower heads rising up from winter slumber to greet the sun. The name dandelion is believed to stem from the similarity between the plant's jagged leaves and the teeth of a lion. Likewise, the dandelion's long, incisor-like tap roots look equally toothy when dug out and extracted from the soil. Many folks consider it a weed, but we positively welcome it into our garden – you can make tasty tea and a cracking cup of coffee from this tenacious, lawn-loving plant.

FORAGE IT

Forage your dandelions in springtime for tender shoots and newly emerged flowers. Autumn hunting is best for gathering large, pendulous roots to turn into coffee. Dig down deep with a trowel to maximize your haul.

GROW IT

Gardeners with a slack approach to lawn care will undoubtedly have a limitless supply of dandelions to call on, but if you do feel the need to cultivate them, dig and chop up pieces of root and sow them on the surface of a plant pot filled with compost, covering them with a fine layer of soil. Should you develop an insatiable appetite for dandelion you can cultivate them into huge Frankensteinian specimens. Manure the plants copiously and earth up the lower leaves to stimulate growth. Think Audrey II from *Little Shop of Horrors*, but with a smiley yellow face.

BREW IT

Pluck the petals from a handful of flower heads and steep in boiling water for 5–10 minutes. For a speedier dandelion fix, you can dunk whole flower heads into your mug, but expect a slightly bitter beverage. For a leafy brew, gather and dry young dandelion leaves. Use 1 tsp per cup and leave to infuse for 5 minutes. The undisputed king of dandelion brews can be made from the root. Head on over to *page 168* for our Dandelion Coffee recipe.

HEALTH BENEFITS

According to the law of the school playground, the merest flick from a dandelion will cause the unlucky recipient to wet the bed. This childish superstition is not without merit as in traditional medicine, dandelions are considered a useful diuretic and are also used for treating heart problems, high blood pressure and diseases of the liver and kidney. Flowers are also taken by folk suffering from a cold.

BLEND IT

You'll spot dandelion leaves and flowers cropping up in numerous commercially available, healthy blends. We've combined them with other 'weeds' in our Wild Garden Tea (see *page 123*).

DID YOU KNOW?

The dandelion's pant-wetting potential has blessed it with many regional nicknames. Our favourites include: piss-i-beds (Humberside), *pissenlit* (France) and bumpipes (Scotland).

SOME SURPRISING USES FOR DANDELIONS

Drink!
As well as making fine hot beverages, dandelions can also be used in booze-making. In times of hop shortages, brewers would often turn to dandelion leaves to provide bittering and flavour, while makers of country wines have long claimed that the flowers produce one of the finest tipples.

Eat!
Most of the dandelion is edible, from the roots to the flowers, but the milky stalks are off limits as they contain toxins that cause illness in some people.* Its young leaves are perhaps the most appetising – in fact you'll find them tucked among chervil, endives and a variety of lettuce leaves in mesclun, a tasty and tender green salad that hails from Provence.

Drive!
One of the most unusual uses of dandelions is currently being explored by German tyre manufacturer Continental. Dandelion roots contain a natural rubber and the company hopes that this will provide a sustainable alternative to the current, environmentally unfriendly components.

* We have heard of dandelion stalk juice being squirted onto warts in the hope they miraculously disappear, but along with other wart 'cures' such as banana peel, potatoes and garlic, success seems very unlikely.

Rosemary

(Salvia rosmarinus)

Rosemary is a herb with a unique aroma and flavour. We might describe it as being piney, savoury, slightly bitter, a touch peppery and with even a hint of lemony sharpness but, whatever that flavour, it's great in drinks. We use it frequently in beer and as a cocktail garnish besides, of course, dunking it in hot water for tea.

GROW IT

Rosemary is native to warmer regions of the world – the Mediterranean, Asia and parts of North America – but it's fairly hardy and only fails in extremely cold spots. Besides warmth its main requirement is drainage, so if your soil is on the heavy side then dig in some horticultural grit before planting. It's an evergreen plant and can be regularly trimmed throughout spring and summer with new growth constantly replenishing the plant. Go easy on cutting back in winter as it will need its strength to survive the cold rather than produce new shoots.

BREW IT

Rosemary's flavour intensity can vary throughout the year, but generally 2 freshly plucked sprigs are ample for a cup of tea. We like the instant freshness of newly picked sprigs, but it also dries well – use 1 tsp per cup of boiling water. If you're looking to impress, sprinkle a few of its soft purple flowers onto the water's surface.

HEALTH BENEFITS

Rosemary is noted for its ability to improve 'prospective memory' (remembering to do something in the future, like returning this book to the library perhaps) with the hope being that it could eventually help to prevent dementia. There are several other medicinal claims made about the herb but we've forgotten what they are.

BLEND IT

Besides other herbs we think it pairs well with tart and citrussy flavours like hibiscus and orange.

Lavender

(Lavandula angustifolia)

Wander past a lavender bush in summer and it's hard to resist breathing in a little deeper for a lungful of its soothing, perfumed aroma. Just a couple of flower heads is all it takes to export that fragrance to a mug of hot liquid, allowing you to recreate that relaxing summer scent wherever you are.

GROW IT

These days garden centres are stocked with a huge range of fancy lavenders, from the frilly butterfly looks of French lavender to varieties that come in white and pink, but for culinary purposes it's the old-fashioned purple 'Common' or 'English' lavender you should seek out (*Lavandula angustifolia*). Growing from seed can be slow and erratic, and larger plants are often very pricey, but it's easy to propagate from cuttings and small potted plants will grow quickly, reaching full size in 2–3 years.

Like most Mediterranean plants they like sun and good drainage, so add some grit to claggy soil and plant on a slight mound if you can. Trim the soft growth after flowering to keep it in shape or leave alone to grow wild and woody.

BREW IT

A little lavender goes a long way – just 2–3 flower heads (or 1 tsp of dried flowers) will be enough for a mug of hot water. Dry the flower heads still attached to their stalks – you can tie them in bunches and suspend them in a warm room – and then pick the flowers off before storing.

You can drink lavender tea on its own but we find it much more effective to add its aromatic charms to another hot drink. Its soothing skills are even more noticeable when working in tandem with milk, so add some to a milky black tea, chai, latté or just a mug of hot milk.

HEALTH BENEFITS

The calming fragrance of lavender has long been used by aromatherapists to help treat anxiety and some people use it to ease a headache.

BLEND IT

Lavender is often combined with other calming herbs, such as lemon balm, and regularly features in floral blends. We like it simply infused into black tea – sprinkle a few teaspoons of flowers into a 250 g (8 oz) packet of loose tea and allow them to work their magic for a couple of days before brewing.

LAVENDER SUGAR

A great way to get your lavender fix in teas (or biscuits, cakes and desserts) is to make lavender sugar. Simply mix a couple of teaspoons of lavender flowers into 250 g (8 oz) of caster sugar and allow them to infuse for a few days before using.

Hyssop

(Hyssopus officinalis)

This herbaceous perennial is a relative of mint and has a menthol flavouring that certainly reminds us of its family friend. But it also brings its own unique characteristics, possessing an unusually spicy, bitter edge that makes it terrific for teas. Its shrubby, evergreen good looks are well suited to garden borders and the bees love it too, with apiarists using it to produce an intense honey that could just be the perfect sweetener for your healthy drinks.

GROW IT

Hyssop is easy to cultivate from seed and grows quite quickly, eventually becoming a small shrub with woody stems. It likes well-drained soil and a spot of sunshine, and is rarely troubled by pests. Its spikes of flowers are commonly a purply blue, but can also be pink, red or white. Not to be confused with anise hyssop (see *page 114*).

BREW IT

You can make tea from hyssop's leaves and flowers, although we only use the former, saving the flowers for our insect friends instead. The leaves are tiny, so you'll need a fair few, fresh or dry, to fill 1 tsp for a cup of tea. Just fill the cup with hot water and, for some additionally invigorating freshness, a squeeze of lemon juice.

HEALTH BENEFITS

Hyssop has something of a medicinal smell,* so it's not surprising it has been a common ingredient in various remedies for centuries. Its main use has been to stave off impending colds, while some folk also take it to clear their phlegmy passages once a cold has struck. It has been claimed to be good for (among other things) the digestive system, blood flow, as a calming aid, an immune system booster, and a treatment for cuts, sores, bites and stings. If all this is true, then you can have an entire medicine cabinet in just one plant.

BLEND IT

Hyssop's punchy flavours and medicinal aromas make it a good alternative (or partner) to mint in healthy herbal concoctions.

DID YOU KNOW?

Hyssop is a key ingredient in several herbal liqueurs, notably Chartreuse and Bénédictine, while its aromatic charms are also put to good use in eau de colognes.

---

* *In centuries gone by, it was used like an ancient form of bleach to clean rooms that had a whiff of sickness to them. And even further back in time, it was used as a holy herb to purge the souls of wrongdoing.*

Nettle

(*Urtica dioica*)

Nettle can be one of the most frustrating plants for foragers. It's abundant, versatile, delicious and nutritious, but grab a handful in passing and you'll be covered in painful stings. It's worth the extra effort of tackling the venomous weed with gloves and scissors – you can harvest a whole load of leaves in no time and make one of the most popular wild teas around.

FORAGE IT

Nettles love the UK's cool, damp climate, but are adaptable enough to attempt world domination, growing just about everywhere. They usually cover large areas, particularly on the edges of cultivated land, and the leaves are at their best when they emerge in spring.

BREW IT

The leaves' tannic astringency and green vitality make a tea that instantly tastes healthy and refreshing. Young leaves are best, so pick in early spring or use the tips (the top two sets of leaves) later in the year. Just 2–3 fresh tips, steeped in boiling water for 5 minutes, make a great cup of tea. The leaves are also excellent dried* – their flavours significantly intensify and just 1 tsp, steeped for 5 minutes, is enough for a tea.

HEALTH BENEFITS

Nettles are chock-full of minerals and nutrients, including iron and vitamin C, making the tea a healthy and invigorating tonic. Among its apparent benefits are a treatment for hay fever (and other allergies), boosting immunity, reducing blood sugar, treating anaemia and detoxifying kidneys. If only they provided a cure for stings...

WHITE DEAD NETTLE

Nettle's stingless lookalike has bright white flowers clustered around its leaves and is also suitable for tea-making. Again, it's the tips you need and you can also include the flowers.
If you're eagerly foraging before the flowers are out, there are two ways of telling it apart from the stinging nettle:

1. Look at the stems: the dead nettle's are square and hollow, the stinging nettle's are round and solid.

2. Grab a handful...

BLEND IT

Those tannins in the dried leaves are excellent for a wide variety of teas and go with most other ingredients. You'll commonly find them in healthy herbal blends.

* *Be careful when drying your own, for even a crispy dry nettle leaf can sting.*

DID YOU KNOW?

The nettle's sting is caused by a combination of neurotransmitters and acids at the tips of its hairy leaves. Some nettle-based oddness occurs every year in Dorset, England, where a pub holds the World Nettle Eating Championships in which competitors see who can eat the most leaves.

Lemon Verbena

(Aloysia citrodora)

This large, deciduous shrub of South America is arguably the king of lemon-scented plants (actual lemon trees aside). Lemon verbena's strong lemon smell is down to the essential oils that reside in its leaves. Try rubbing a fresh leaf between your finger and thumb and give it a good sniff – it's like sticking your nose in a big bag of lemon sherbet sweets, an aroma that transfers magnificently well to wild tea.

GROW IT

Lemon verbena is a rather tender plant – if yours live in the ground, mulch and protect them from frosts. Place potted plants in the greenhouse from late autumn. If your plant appears skeletal and lifeless after winter, hold back from hurling it towards the compost bin as new growth takes time to appear and it may well rise Lazarus-like in late spring.

BREW IT

Use 3–4 freshly picked leaves per cup of boiled water, bruising them first before dropping them in. Essential oils held in the leaves help this herb to retain its zingy lemon taste, which becomes even stronger after air drying – try using 1–2 tsp of dried leaves per cup.

HEALTH BENEFITS

Lemon verbena has long been used as a mild sedative; its high antioxidant properties have been known to reduce muscle damage during exercise. Try filling your water bottle with cold lemon verbena tea for your morning run – it might help ease your achy legs and joints.

BLEND IT

Fresh leaves add a citrussy punch to iced teas, while the dried leaves are excellent for injecting lemon flavour into blends in place of actual lemons.

MORE LEMONY PLANTS TO TRY

Lemon Balm (*Melissa officinalis*)
A large-leafed lemon-scented herb, perfect for tea-making purposes (see *opposite*).

Lemongrass (*Cymbopogon citratus*)
Its edible stems are widely used in oriental cuisine and the leaves make a great tea (see *page 108*). It likes hot climes and hates frosts.

Lemon Basil (*Ocimum × citriodorum*)
A hybrid of American basil and sweet basil. Infuse it in olive oil for a flavoursome dipping oil for crusty bread. Nick declares this variety his favourite basil for tea-making.

Lemon Balm

(Melissa officinalis)

This bushy, rampant perennial belongs to the mint family. You'll often spy it lurking in kitchen gardens where it is grown to lend lemony flavours to savoury dishes, salads and sauces. As well as boasting excellent culinary credentials, lemon balm has enjoyed a long association with beekeepers. Bees can't get enough of this zesty plant, so it has historically been placed near beehives to placate the apian inhabitants and to hopefully prevent them from swarming off to pastures new. The clue is in the name: *Melissa officinalis* stems from the Greek word *melissa*, meaning 'honeybee'.

GROW IT

Lemon balm loves most soil types and will grow happily in shade or full sun. It's quite invasive, so keep it in check by cutting back the plant after it flowers. This will also encourage fresh growth, which makes the best tea. If things get really out of hand and it starts to swamp surrounding plants, lift and divide clumps in autumn.

BREW IT

The leaves of lemon balm tend to lose aroma when dried, so if you have easy access to a plant use them fresh, harvesting just before the plant starts to bear flowers for maximum fragrance. Try infusing 2 tsp of leaves in a mug full of freshly boiled water for 5–10 minutes.

HEALTH BENEFITS

Lemon balm contains eugenol, an aromatic, oily liquid that has both anaesthetic and antiseptic qualities. You may find it stuffed into hop pillows, along with lavender, chamomile and the obligatory hop to aid and improve sleep for people who suffer from insomnia.

BLEND IT

Try mixing fresh lemon balm leaves with some of its minty mates. Our preferred pairing is with peppermint, where it brings a fresh citric zip to proceedings. Folks with a sweet tooth should add a spoonful of honey in homage to this bee-loved balm.

DID YOU KNOW?

Not all insects are as enamoured with lemon balm as bees. Mosquitoes positively hate it, so gardeners who are regularly pestered by these biting blighters should rub a crushed handful of leaves over exposed skin to keep them at bay.

Chamomile

(*Matricaria recutita*)

Chamomile is a herbal tea trailblazer, and was available in supermarkets and health food shops long before most other wild brews got in on the act. If you want to grow your own then there are two types you're likely to encounter, German chamomile (*Matricaria recutita*) and Roman chamomile (*Chamaemelum nobile*). Roman chamomile is the low-lying, ragged-looking one (also known as the ground apple) and the one you need to choose if you fancy planting a fragrant (yet maintenance heavy) chamomile lawn. It's the German variety that we've had the most success with on our allotment. It also happens to be the one most widely used for medicinal purposes and, more importantly, the best for making tasty tea.

FORAGE IT

German chamomile is native to southern and eastern Europe and western Asia. You'll be lucky to find any German chamomile on your UK foraging excursions, but you may well stumble across Roman chamomile. It used to be prevalent in the UK, but now tends to be confined to a few areas in the south of England. It's a threatened species, so if you happen to come across any in the wild, leave it well alone.

GROW IT

Chamomile will grow well from seed, which is best started in trays, with the young seedlings transplanted into the garden when big enough to handle. Both Roman and German chamomile are quite adaptable to most growing conditions, but the German chamomile tends to be a

bit more rugged and will grow quite happily in poorer soil conditions. Unlike its ground hugging Roman cousin, German chamomile stands upright and can reach heights of over 60 cm (24 in). Clip your plants regularly during the growing season to prevent them from becoming leggy and keep them well watered to prevent drying out.

BREW IT

You can use either fresh or dried flowers, but using fresh will give you a fruitier brew, plus you'll get an instant fix without the faff of drying. Don't overdo it, as too many flowers will make a bitter beverage. Try using 3–4 flower heads in a cup of hot water for starters and see how you get on. Let them infuse for 5 minutes, strain, then sup.

DID YOU KNOW?

Chamomile tea can be used as a face wash to help treat acne. Just use the tea recipe left, remembering to LET IT COOL FIRST.

HEALTH BENEFITS

Chamomile tea is highly prized for its reported calming properties. Some folk also take it to relax their muscles and to ease aches and pains, making it a favourite beverage for gardeners to glug after a hard day's graft.

BLEND IT

Try blending chamomile as part of a floral blend. Lavender works well, as does a rose petal/green tea combo. Adding lemon balm helps bring out the fruity flavours – and smells incredible to boot.

Bee Balm

(Monarda didyma)

Bee balm is one of the many names given to monarda, a striking herbaceous plant that possesses bee-alluring pollen. Another of its aliases* is bergamot, because its leaves possess an aroma similar to the bergamot fruit. It's this latter quality that earns it a place in our top 40 and, although you can also use the flowers for tea, we prefer to leave them to the bees and plunder the greenery instead.

GROW IT

There are annual bee balm plants out there, but we're devoting our attention to the perennial *Monarda didyma*. Although it shouldn't be too difficult to grow, we've found it to be one of those fussy plants that will decide it doesn't want to bother for seemingly no reason. It likes to be kept watered in good, well-drained soil, but will throw a tantrum if it dries out (in summer) or sits in excessive water (especially over winter). It likes a bit of space to grow, but after a few years will spread to the point where it needs to be dug up and split into smaller plants. Deadhead flowers in summer to extend the blooming season, then cut the plant to the ground in autumn. A bit of spring mulch will get it up and running again.

BREW IT

Bee balm's leaves have an unusual aromatic orange fragrance, similar to the bergamot fruit, along with some herby qualities, with thyme most coming to mind. We think its aromas and flavours are enhanced by drying the leaves, but you can also use them fresh. Either way, 1–2 tsp of chopped leaves added to a cup of boiling water and steeped for at least 5 minutes makes a good tea.

HEALTH BENEFITS

Monarda didyma hails from North America and has been a traditional remedy for skin and mouth-related ailments among Native Americans as the plant contains thymol, an ingredient that regularly features in mouth washes. It has also been used by some folk in their own personal battles with flatulence.

BLEND IT

Those bergamot similarities see it used as an alternative to the fruit's oil in an approximation of Earl Grey (see page 125) and you can also mix it with lemon and orange peel to enhance those citrussy characteristics.

TOP TIP

Bee balm benefits from a 'Chelsea chop' – the hacking back of some plants post-Chelsea Flower Show (late May) to encourage more vigorous growth. Lop off the top two-thirds of your bee balm plants and turn the leaves into a stockpile of dried tea.

* Another alias is Oswego Tea, on account of it being a popular drink among Oswego Indians.

Pot Marigold

(Calendula officinalis)

Pot marigold seems to have fallen out of gardening fashion, frequently overlooked in favour of showier cultivars of French and African marigolds (from the *Tagetes* genus). But these fancier flowers lack one key feature for us – they're not edible – so it's the simpler sunshine colours of the pot marigold that brightens up our allotment and adds a splash of colour to our teas.

GROW IT

There are loads of *Calendula officinalis* varieties available in a full range of sunny colours, from vibrant yellows to deep oranges (and with a few pale peachy pinks for good measure), but it's worth tracking down the original 'pot marigold', which has a vivid mid-orange hue. Sowing this annual from its squiggly-looking seed is easy (a successful crop is likely to self-seed for the following year), and a healthy plant should flower from early summer through to the first frosts. It looks good in pots as well as in borders.

BREW IT

You can make tea with the leaves and green parts of the flowers, but they can be an irritant to the throat, so it's best to stick with the petals. If you're drying them, pick the whole flowers and pluck the petals when they've fully dried out. On their own, the petals make a delicious but delicate brew, so infuse 1 2 tsp (fresh or dried) for at least 5 minutes in a cup of hot water. It could be a psychological thing, but we think the yellow strands not only look like saffron but taste a bit like it too, with a slightly sweet and earthy flavour.

HEALTH BENEFITS

Pot marigold has antibacterial properties and has traditionally been used to treat skin ailments, such as burns, bites, stings and itchy irritations, but we don't advise pouring a mug of hot tea over any such sores. Instead, drinking it is said to provide healthy nourishment to your skin and is used to help ease a sore throat.

BLEND IT

Those delicate flavours make it hard for pot marigold to shine in any tea blends, although it does often appear in floral brews, especially those devised for their health benefits.

DID YOU KNOW?

Marigold petals have long been used in cooking as a colourful saffron substitute and to provide a yellow tinge to foodstuffs such as cheese and butter. They are also used to thicken and flavour pots of soup and stews – it's for this reason the plant got its 'pot' marigold name.

Wild Fennel

(*Foeniculum vulgare*)

If you like the taste of aniseed then grow some fennel. Every part of this magnificent plant – leaves, flowers, seeds, stalks and roots – is infused with its flavour, and hot water is all you need to add for a mug of aniseedy goodness. But the perennial herb is not only packed with flavour, it also has great visual appeal, with a vast web of lush green fronds in spring, followed by masses of yellow flowers in summer.

GROW IT

Fennel is a member of the carrot family and there are two edible types you can grow.* Florence fennel is cultivated for its bulbs, which swell while growing, although we've found it a bit of a fussy plant on our patch and rarely get much girth before it bolts. Instead, we grow the much larger and more spectacular wild fennel, also known as herb fennel or common fennel.

It's best sown in situ early in the year and is easy to grow (although given the choice it will opt for sunshine and well-drained soil). Plants can reach up to 3 m (9.8 ft) tall, so it will hog a large corner of your garden, but it's such a handsome looking plant that it's well worth giving up the space.

FORAGE IT

Due to its bullying size and the ease at which it self-seeds, fennel is often seen as an unwanted invader when it appears in the wild. If you're out on a fennel foraging mission. then your best bet is to hunt around recently broken areas of ground, roadside verges or sites close to the coast.

* A similar plant, *giant fennel* (Ferula communis), *can be poisonous, while another carrot relative, rock samphire* (Crithmum maritimum), *is also known as sea fennel.*

BREW IT

You could try digging up the roots to brew with, but it's a lot of effort for minimum rewards when there's a vast plant on top that comes back year after year to give you lots of tea-making opportunities. The seeds are the highlight, with 1 tsp surrendering plenty of flavour when infused in a mug of hot water for at least 5 minutes (lightly crack them first with a pestle and mortar for maximum effect). Before the seeds are ready, you can steep the frilly fronds in a cup of hot water for 5–10 minutes – simply grab a small handful (stems included) and roughly chop before infusing.

HEALTH BENEFITS

Fennel is most commonly used as a digestive aid and appears in numerous concoctions promoting women's health, with attention given to its supposed abilities to ease period pains. It's also found in teas designed for new mums as it is said to help increase their production of breast milk (see *page 129*).

BLEND IT

Fennel seeds are a versatile ingredient for the wild tea maker, working particularly well in spicy drinks (see our chai recipes on *page 130*), or for adding some sweet aniseed flavours to herbal brews.

WHEN TO HARVEST SEEDS

In late autumn, the fennel seeds (technically the plant's fruit) will begin to ripen. The best time to pick them is when their green colour has faded and begins to show light shades of brown (if you leave them too long they'll get browner and start to fall off or go soggy when rained upon). Pick the whole flower head, rub the seeds into a bowl and remove any bits of stalky debris (and bugs) before storing in an airtight container.

Echinacea

(Echinacea angustifolia, Echinacea purpurea)

Echinacea is a herbaceous plant that has been used as a medicinal tea by Native Americans for centuries; it is commonly known as purple coneflower in the US (although not all varieties are purple). Its large blooms sit on tall, sturdy stems, which has made it as popular in flower borders as in the medicine cabinet. Grow it yourself and you'll have to wrestle with the conundrum of whether to enjoy its visual delights or chop it up and drink it instead.

GROW IT

There are many echinacea varieties, cultivars and hybrids but tea makers should stick to the two most commonly used in medicine: *Echinacea angustifolia* and *Echinacea purpurea*. It likes conditions akin to those found in the American prairies where it grows wild – hot and bare – so give it your sunniest spot and try not to overcrowd it with other plants. It will also need plenty of room below ground for its deep roots to burrow, making it less effective in pots. Established plants can be divided in spring or autumn to increase your stock.

BREW IT

It's echinacea's roots that are most commonly used, but you can also make teas from the leaves, flowers and seeds. It seems a shame to dig up plants to harvest the roots, especially as cleaning and preparing them is fiddly, so we stick to the leaves. Steep 1 tsp of leaves in a cup of boiling water for 5 minutes to make the tea. The most noticeable property of echinacea tea is the tingling sensation it gives your tongue. We think it's more suited to blends than drinking on its own.

HEALTH BENEFITS

Echinacea was something of a super-herb for Native Americans who traditionally used it to treat a myriad of ailments, from sore throats and toothache to scorpion stings and snakebites. These days it has become a general wellbeing remedy that's used in all sorts of flu and cold potions.

BLEND IT

It works well with other floral teas (it will benefit from their aroma, while they'll appreciate echinacea's earthy and tongue-tingling properties) and with other cold-fighting ingredients such as rose hips and elderberries, which come packed with vitamin C (see *page 129*).

DID YOU KNOW?

The genus name *Echinacea* is derived from the Greek word for 'hedgehog' (*ekhinos*) because the flower's centre looks like the spiny mammal.

Sweetcorn

(Zea mays)

Sweetcorn is one of the best vegetables to grow yourself. Few things taste as good as a ripe cob freshly snapped from its stalk and plunged straight into boiling water or put onto a barbecue. If only there was something you could do with the cob's flowing mane of corn silks. Well actually there is...

GROW IT

Sweetcorn is a reliable grower from seed and, providing your plants get ample sun and water, you should get little trouble from them. Sweetcorn uses the wind to pollinate, so it needs to be planted in blocks – if you grow it in a row and the wind blows in the wrong direction, your cobs will be cornless. You also have to keep an eye out for other mammals snaffling the goods – badgers will trash an entire crop to get at those golden ears, while rodents' stealthier approach can strip the sweet niblets from a cob in no time.

BREW IT

A tea made from roasted corn is popular in Korea. It involves cooking the kernels in boiling water for just a few minutes, then thoroughly drying them before slowly roasting until they are almost black. These are then ground and used as a tea – it's so popular in Korea that you can readily buy roasted corn tea bags.

For a much simpler brew, you can also use the corn silks – the hairy tassels that flow from each ear.* You can wrench the corn silks from the cobs once the kernels have started to turn golden yellow and use them fresh or dried. Simply trim away any brown or ratty looking ends and put 1 tbsp of fresh silks (when scrunched up) or 2 tsp of dried silks in a mug and cover with boiling water for 2–3 minutes. The tea has a sweet and mild corn-like flavour that you may wish to pep up with a sliver of ginger.

HEALTH BENEFITS

Corn silks have been used as a traditional medicine in some countries for centuries, due to the belief that they have diuretic properties that can flush the system of toxins and help with urinary and kidney problems (although there doesn't seem to be a whole lot of substantiated research available to back this up).

BLEND IT

We think corn silk is best used as a background flavour for brews with spices such as ginger, or it can be blended with Roasted Barley Tea (see page 144) to add some sweetness to the more bitter barley.

* The Latin name for corn silks is Stigmata maydis, which means 'mother's hair'. This, and 'ear hair', don't sound as appetising to us as 'corn silks'.

Oats

(*Avena sativa*)

Oats are an odd choice to have growing on an allotment, we'll grant you that. You'll most likely spy oats sprouting in vast fields on an industrial scale, destined to be pummelled into porridge, or made into animal fodder to feed hungry ruminants. Down on the plot, we've surrendered a raised bed for their cultivation. They make a fine sight, swaying in the breeze under the soft, golden glow of a late summer sun, but our real interest lies in beverages. Our oats are grown for beer-making experiments and to provide us with the necessary ingredients for a tasty, wholesome cuppa.

GROW IT

Oats are an annual plant and can be sown either in autumn (for a late summer harvest) or in the spring (for an early autumn harvest). Sow the seeds in shallow rows, or use the tried and trusted, old-school method of scattering them randomly with a flick of the wrist. Lightly cover the area with soil or run the risk of birds hoovering up your seeds before they germinate. Oat grows vigorously and densely, so you shouldn't have many problems with weeds once established.

When growing for maximum yield, farmers will harvest the oat grains just after the last green kernels start to turn cream. Overripe grain tends to detach easily from the plant and you'll lose a lot to the soil when gathering mechanically on an industrial scale. For tea-making purposes, you'll need the whole plant (bar the roots) so you don't need to be so precise with timings – wait until the grains have turned golden and harvest using a sharp knife, cutting the plant a couple of centimetres above soil level.

BREW IT

Oats need a bit of coaxing to release their goodness. Chop up a couple of handfuls of oats (leaves, stems and kernels), pour over boiling water, and steep overnight. In the morning, reheat your oaty brew in a saucepan, then pour it through a strainer into a cup. Oat kernels alone can be used to make a tasty milk alternative (see *page 24*)

HEALTH BENEFITS

One of the major benefits of eating oats is that they lower cholesterol, thanks to the soluble fibre they contain. Oat straw tea is also believed to be a brain-booster that can improve mental performance. They are also full of melatonin which can make you sleepy – just ask Goldilocks...

BLEND IT

We think oats work well with lemony additions, so give them a go with lemon verbena or lemon balm. Oat straw and mint also make an interesting combination.

DID YOU KNOW?

Oats are the staple grain of Scotland, as unlike fussy old wheat, they thrive in the country's cold, wet and humid climate. See also whisky and midges.

Rose

(Rosa)

With edible flowers and fruits, a rose bush can provide rich pickings for the thirsty gardener. As a general rule, petals plucked from the more fragrant varieties are often the best for turning into tea. An obvious and aptly named candidate for the pot is the tea rose, as its spicy fragrance is similar to that of black tea. We also make fine floral brews from the fruits – the dog rose (*Rosa canina*) being one of our favourites. We once regarded this as an unwelcome allotment guest, because of its tendency to entangle our precious hop bines. We now spare it a savaging from our shears and welcome our new brewing buddy with open arms.

FORAGE IT

The dog rose is the variety you'll most likely come across when out foraging. It's also known as the wild rose, and it'll be positively furious when you start picking its petals. Don't bag them all for yourself – leave a few flower heads on the plant for insects to enjoy. Make a mental note of the location of the plants you discover, as you may wish to return later in the year to gather rose hips for more brewing action or to make rosehip syrup for bubble tea (see *page 166*).

GROW IT

Roses are pretty hardy and will thrive in most soil conditions. They like plenty of sunshine and are not too keen on windy sites. They can be thirsty fellas, so keep them well watered to promote healthy growth and to prolong the flowering period. Deadheading your roses is an essential

(and a rather satisfying) part of healthy plant management. Go around your bush after the flowers have finished blooming and snip off any dead heads with a sharp pair of secateurs – you can cut back each flowering stem as far as three sets of leaves. Hip-sters who are looking forward to foraging rosehips should skip the deadheading and allow the fruits to form in peace.

BREW THE PETALS

A tea made solely from rose petals smells great but is quite subtle on the palate, so it's best to blend them with green or black tea leaves to bring out those floral flavours (see Tea Twists, *page 125*).

BREW THE HIPS

Rosehips are the real star of the show and pack stacks of vitamin C, making them the perfect fruity addition to a healthy brew (see *page 128*). Roughly

chop and dry the fruits, add 1 tsp to a cup and fill with hot water, then leave to infuse for 5–10 minutes. Make sure you strain the tea thoroughly before serving as the tiny hairs found inside rosehips can irritate the throat.

HEALTH BENEFITS

The health-giving properties of the rose are not to be sniffed at. Rose tea is high in vitamin C, which can stimulate the production of the white blood cells that play a key role in fighting infections.

BLEND IT

Hawthorn leaves and wild rose petals make a refreshing, lightly floral brew; try a 3 to 1 mix (in favour of the rose petal). Dried and ground rose hips can add fruity flavours to any number of healthy tonics.

Ginger

(Zingiber officinale)

Ginger is an indispensable ingredient for the aspiring drinks maker. A native of South East Asia, the plant in the wild produces elegant, cone-like flowers. The part we are concerned with, however, is the root — the technically inaccurate name given to the knobbly, hand-shaped rhizome from which the plant's stems sprout.

GROW IT

Growing ginger is a protracted affair — to be honest, you are probably better off foraging it from your local supermarket. It can be done, though, if you are prepared to be patient. Go to the shops and select a piece of ginger, ideally one that already has small green buds forming. Give it a wash, cut off the bit with the bud and place in a tall pot filled with gritty compost on a sunny windowsill. Green shoots should start to appear in a few weeks, and after a good 6–8 months you should notice a bulbous swelling where the shoots meet the soil. This is the rhizome, and the part which we crave. Eventually the foliage of your plants will die down and you can harvest the root, although you may wish to let the plant develop larger rhizomes and pick them the following year. Dry the root somewhere dark and cool until its outer skin turns papery, remembering to save some back to continue the growing cycle.

BREW IT

Shred 45 g (1½ oz) of fresh ginger root into a cup, add boiling water to fill the cup and allow to steep for 10 minutes. Strain before serving, adding a slice of lemon and honey to taste.

HEALTH BENEFITS

Ginger has long been used as a treatment for an upset stomach and many people take it as a cure for travel sickness. It also contains powerful anti-inflammatory compounds called gingerols, which can help soothe sore muscles and joints.

BLEND IT

Ginger has a tendency to boss whatever it is paired with so use it sparingly or fight fire with fire and combine it with a nip or two of chilli powder for a real zinger of a brew. It's a common feature of winter warming brews and spicy chais (see *page 130*) and also works well with sharply flavoured ingredients such as lemon and rhubarb (see *page 167*). It's also handy for taming the taste of some of the more challenging brews, such as Bladder Wrack Tea (see *page 94*).

GINGER TEAS

Sliced, grated or peeled? Everyone has a favourite way of making ginger tea. Here are three regional varieties to try:

TEH HALIA
Malaysia

1 Peel and bruise a 2.5 cm (1 in) piece of ginger.
2 Boil 1 cup of water in a small pan, add the ginger and simmer for 10 minutes.
3 Remove the ginger from the pan, remove the pan from the heat and add 1 tsp of black tea.
4 Leave to brew for 5 minutes, strain then add a dash of condensed milk to serve.

SAENGGANG-CHA
Korea

1 Peel and thinly slice a 2.5 cm (1 in) piece of ginger.
2 Boil 1 cup of water in a small pan, add the sliced ginger, half a cinnamon stick and simmer for 20 minutes.
3 Strain into a cup, sweeten with honey and serve with pine nuts.

ADRAK KI CHAI
India

1 Peel and finely grate a 2.5 cm (1 in) piece of ginger.
2 Mix ½ a cup of milk and ½ a cup of water together in a pan and bring to a boil.
3 Add the grated ginger and simmer for 5 minutes.
4 Add 1 tsp strong black tea, turn off the heat and brew for 5 minutes.
5 Serve with honey to taste.

Lemon

(Citrus limon)

The sharp, acidic bite of lemon can cut through all flavours, lending its zesty refreshment to a number of hot and cold drinks. With its versatility ranging from classic lemon tea to a soothing honey and lemon mix or invigorating lemon and ginger, everyone should make sure they always have a lemon or two to hand.

GROW IT

We don't live in the best part of the world for lemon growing, as they like sun and warmth throughout the year. It's possible to grow them outdoors in summer and bring them into a heated greenhouse or conservatory during the winter, but we lack those facilities so rely on shop bought imports instead. Make sure to wash off any wax coatings in warm water before using them.

BREW IT

There are many ways to add a burst of zesty lemon freshness to drinks: a squirt of juice straight into a cup, a slice as a flavoursome garnish, or adding dried zest to a blend (see boxout, right, for ideas). For the simplest, purest lemon tea, simply steep 2 slices in a cup of hot water for 5 minutes and serve hot or ice cold.

HEALTH BENEFITS

Lemon's most well-known health benefit is its abundance of antioxidants – notably vitamin C – which are more concentrated in the zest and pith. Start drinking it if cold bugs are circulating in your vicinity and it might just help to prevent them from striking.

BLEND IT

There aren't many ingredients that kick up a fuss when asked to share a mug with lemon. Besides the classics listed in our boxout, below, its acidity is also useful for adding character to simple floral teas such as elderflower or bringing out even more flavour from fruity brews.

FIVE WAYS WITH LEMON

The classic: Squeeze 1-2 tsp of fresh lemon juice into a cup of black tea (refrigerate for an iced tea).

The soother: Combine 2 tsp of lemon juice with 2 tsp of honey in a cup then fill with hot water.

The invigorator: Chop a thumb-tip size piece of ginger and drop into a cup of hot water with a few slices of lemon

The refresher: Add a couple of slices of lemon to a mug of mint tea.

The pick-me-up: The Portuguese drink *mazagran* is made by squeezing the juice from ½ a lemon into a cup of black coffee and sweetening it with 2 tsp of sugar. Best served chilled with ice.

Strawberries

(Fragaria)

Speak to an allotmenteer and they will tell you that no shop-bought veg or fruit will ever compare to the taste of their own, fresh grown produce. While this may not be the case for all home-grown foodstuffs, there's nothing quite like the taste of home-grown strawberries. They are the very essence of British summertime distilled into a red, fruity package. They also happen to make pretty tasty teas.

FORAGE IT

Unless you inadvertently wander through a fruit farm while out foraging, you are unlikely to come across the cultivated varieties you'll find on supermarket shelves (for growing tips on these, see below). What you may well find is the wild, alpine strawberry (*Fragaria vesca*, pictured below), a small, ground-hugging plant that produces equally diminutive fruits. Don't be fooled by their size – its strawberries have an intense, punchy flavour and the leaves of the alpine variety are the ones most often used in alternative medicine.

GROW IT

Strawberry plants can be grown from seed but the best (and easiest) option is to buy small plants. Plant them out in early spring, preferably in

well-drained soil in a sunny position. During the summer months, just before your strawberry plants start to bear fruit, it's always good practice to lay down a bed of straw under the plants to help protect the developing fruits from slugs and other critters fond of juicy red snacks. Remove this bedding in late summer to let the plants breathe and reduce the chance of disease, then cut back your strawberry plants to 5 cm (2 in) above the earth. Your plants will then benefit from a generous feed of fertilizer to help them settle down for winter.

BREW IT

Strawberries are perfect for sun teas and also for syrups, which can be used to make a sweet and juicy iced tea. For an instant, delicately fragranced, pale pink cuppa, slice 3–4 ripe strawberries (or a small handful of whole alpine strawberries) and steep them in a cup of boiling water. It takes just a couple of minutes for them to surrender their flavours, and you can also invite a few strawberry leaves or some green tea into the party for extra flavour. Strain and serve hot or cold.

HEALTH BENEFITS

Colourful fruits like the strawberry contain anthocyanins which are believed to have a healthy effect on the heart. Strawberries also contain decent amounts of fibre, potassium and calcium, and their antioxidants may help support the immune system.

BLEND IT

Try adding a touch of vanilla when making a Strawberry Iced Tea (see *page 154*) for a tasty approximation of strawberries and ice cream.

STRAWBERRY YIELDS FOREVER

A continuous supply of strawberry plants can be cultivated from a single specimen by propagating the runners (or stolons). Here's how to do it:

1. Select 2–3 runners closest to the mother plant and pin them down with a tent peg. Weighing them down with a small stone should also do the trick.

2. Once the runners have taken root – which should take around 4–6 weeks – carefully cut the stem from the mother plant and your new plants should begin to thrive on their own.

3. Use this technique to cultivate your strawberry beds in situ, or train individual runners into plant pots to then transport and plant elsewhere.

Apple

(*Malus*)

We live in apple country, surrounded by ancient orchards and a landscape peppered with wild trees that have grown from discarded cores. Between us we grow eight varieties of dessert, culinary and cider apples, which we use for pies, alcohol and juice, while also taking advantage of their sweet nature in a range of tasty teas.

GROW IT

If you've got room in your garden for a tree, make it one of the hundreds of varieties of apple. Aim for a variety well suited to your region and plant during the winter months while it's dormant. The first few years will be fruitless – it's best to snip off the flowers to concentrate growth in the actual tree – and the tree will need careful pruning according to variety, but when properly established apples need little attention.

FORAGE IT

If, like us, you're lucky enough to have apple trees growing wild near you then keep your fingers crossed they're tasty – some are so packed with tannin they'll suck all the moisture from your cheeks, resulting in the most fearsome gurning expression you've ever pulled. To check if they're ripe, give an apple a shake and you should hear the pips rattling – then cut one in half and they will be brown.

BREW IT

Apples are packed with sugar and, when dried, make a rewardingly sweet and fruity addition to many blends. Apple tea is popular in Turkey and is sold simply as dried apple pieces or powdered with black tea as an 'instant' drink, and it often comes flavoured with spices. For your own apple tea infusion you'll need 2 tsp of dried apple steeped in a cup of hot water for at least 5 minutes. Apple blossoms can also be used to make tea and we have included a recipe specifically for peels and cores (see *page 156*).

HEALTH BENEFITS

Apples have a decent number of vitamins and minerals that will ooze out into a tea. Their natural soluble fibre is also good for digestion and can even be useful for people trying to lose weight, as it makes them feel fuller than they are.

BLEND IT

Apple is excellent for adding to any fruit tea blend for some natural sweetness and fruity flavour and is also good with spices such as cinnamon (see *page 122*), nutmeg or rooty liquorice brews.

HOW TO PLANT A FRUIT TREE

1 Plant your fruit tree between November and March, when the plant is dormant.

2 Choose a sunny, preferably sheltered spot and dig a hole, a third wider than the root ball, and around 30 cm (12 in) deep. Square holes are best for establishing roots – a round hole can cause the roots to spiral.

3 Hammer a support stake into the hole, making sure it sits off-centre and leaves room for the tree.

4 Soak the root ball thoroughly, and place in the hole. Backfill the hole and firm the soil down gently over the roots.

5 Attach a tree tie to the stake and trunk.

6 Stand back and admire your lovely tree.

7 Water the tree thoroughly and continue to water at least once a week for the first six months after planting.

Bladder Wrack

(Fucus vesiculosus)

Bladder wrack is a species of seaweed, easily identifiable by the small air pocket sacks positioned on its tendrils, which help it to bob up and down in the ocean. It's a common sight on rocky shorelines, where you can spy it clinging to rocks like slimy Bubble Wrap. To be honest, bladder wrack tea will divide opinion. Some of you will hate it, some of you will loathe it, but bladder wrack is a seafaring superfood, packed to the gills with vitamins and minerals and is ridiculously good for you. Consider this our healthy gift to you...

FORAGE IT

Bladder wrack is best harvested from mid- to late summer when the plant is at its vitamin-packed prime. Extra caution is advised when foraging for seaweed as there is a danger of being cut off by rising tides. Rocks festooned with seaweed can also be extremely slippery – a careless beach forager can easily be wrongfooted and end up taking an unscheduled dip in the sea, or skid over rocks and have flailing limbs rasped by a thousand knobbly barnacles. Make sure you are not harvesting your brackish bounty next to one of those stinking seaside sewage pipes.

BREW IT

Take your seaweed and wash it THOROUGHLY in fresh water. Leave to dry in the sun and turn it frequently to avoid it turning rancid. No one wants rancid seaweed tea. Grind or chop up ½–1 tsp dried, brittle seaweed per cup, allowing it to infuse in a cup of boiling water for 5 minutes.

SEAWEED FERTILIZER

Does the very thought of drinking seaweed tea disgust you? Not to worry, you can make seaweed plant fertilizer and use it to feed plants instead! Liquid seaweed fertilizer contains many nutrients that are beneficial to plants, including nitrogen, phosphate, potassium and magnesium, and making it is easy:

1 Wash your seaweed thoroughly to rid it of salt, sand and sea-borne debris.

2 Heap the seaweed into a bucket and top up with water.

3 Place a lid on the bucket and leave the seaweed to steep for a month.

4 Strain the resulting liquid into airtight containers. Just be wary of the putrid pong that will hit your nostrils when you pop the lid.

5 Add a couple of capfuls of your newly made fertilizer to a watering can and water the base of your plants, being careful not to spill any on the foliage as this may cause scorching. Store your fertilizer somewhere cool and dark, where it should keep for a month or so.

HEALTH BENEFITS

Bladder wrack is packed with healthy
vitamins and minerals including iodine,
which has been extensively used to
treat goitre – an unsightly swelling of
the thyroid gland in the neck caused by
iodine deficiency. The Romans used it to
help soothe joint pains, and it's also rich
in algin which can act as a laxative.

BLEND IT

Bladder wrack tea can be a bit
challenging on its own, so add some
sprigs of mint or a teaspoon of
something spicy to combat its briney
nature. A drop of honey or maple
syrup also helps.

Bay

(Laurus nobilis)

We're keen admirers of bay trees – also known as bay laurel or sweet bay* – for being one of the few exotically spicy ingredients we're able to grow with ease. Their evergreen nature also means we can rely on a year-round harvest. The leaves have a mild spiciness that is great to cook with (it's a common ingredient in garam masala) and their distinctive aroma is especially effective in hot drinks.

GROW IT

Bay is a low-maintenance plant that can be grown as a tree or a shrub, used for hedging, or constrained to a pot, where it's often trimmed into topiary and stuck either side of a front door to make the house look posh. Free food pickers might also find it growing in parks and other public spaces. Be warned that there are some plants with the laurel name that are poisonous, so make sure you know what you're picking. *Laurus nobilis* is the most familiar of the culinary bay laurels to look for.

BREW IT

You can brew a simple bay leaf tea with 3–4 fresh or dry leaves. Put them in a pan with enough water for your chosen mug, bring to the boil and simmer for 5 minutes. Allow to cool sufficiently before straining and drink on its own, with a slice of lemon or a splash of milk. Dried leaves can also be crumbled into blends, working particularly well in chai teas.

HEALTH BENEFITS

Bay leaves have a long list of vitamins and reported health benefits that range from anti-inflammatory properties to curing dandruff. The comforting spicy aromas of bay leaf oil are also popular with aromatherapists** and bay is commonly used for arthritic aches and pains.

BLEND IT

Its subtly spicy aromas and flavours lend themselves well to spiced teas and chais (see *page 130*).

---

* *Not to be confused with sweetbay magnolia.*

** *Those spicy aromas are less popular with bugs – bay leaf oil is often a feature of insect repellents.*

Sage

(Salvia officinalis)

We had our doubts about sage as a quality tea ingredient as its strong savoury flavour has such an association with stuffing that we couldn't imagine drinking it. But it turns out that sage tea tastes great, giving us another reason to regularly pick leaves and peg back the rampaging plants in our gardens.

GROW IT

We've always found sage a hit-and-miss plant. Sometimes it struggles to muster the strength to get established, but try it in a different location and it thrives, rambling over a vast area and smothering anything in its path. Sage is a member of the mint family and there are hundreds of cultivated and wild varieties – some annual, some perennial, some flowering and with leaves in every shade of green you can imagine (and purple or gold). Unfortunately, not all of these are edible so stick to the common garden sage, *Salvia officinalis*.

BREW IT

Try infusing 6–8 fresh leaves, or 2 tsp of dried leaves per cup of hot water.

Besides its savoury herby flavours it also has some bitterness that we think makes it that extra bit tea-worthy.

HEALTH BENEFITS

Ancient Egyptians used sage to aid fertility, but these days it's most commonly known as a potential antioxidant. Some people also believe it can help to reduce anxiety and lower cholesterol. It's a common ingredient in supplements designed to support women going through menopause.

BLEND IT

Our sage advice is to drink it on its own, but you could try adding lemon or a few warming spices such as cinnamon, bay or cloves.

DID YOU KNOW?

For a spectacular member of the *Salvia* family take a look at the bright red flowers of the pineapple sage (or scarlet pineapple), a Mexican native that does indeed smell of pineapple.

Borage
(Borago officinalis)

This hairy, hardy annual hails from the Mediterranean, but has managed to find a foothold and flourish in northern Europe and parts of North America thanks to its tolerance of a variety of soil conditions and climates. If you have the space, borage is a handy herb to have growing on an allotment. Use it as a companion plant, as it will attract a wide variety of pollinating insects which find the striking blue flower heads irresistible. Its leaves also happen to make a tasty, healthy tea. Just be warned – bees love borage so much you may well have to fight them for it.

FORAGE IT
Look for borage in pastures and in deciduous woodland. Its large leaves are similar to other, more unpalatable species but its star-shaped flowers, which hang in downward-facing clusters, are quite distinctive and start to appear from early summer.

GROW IT
Borage can easily be grown from seed and prefers a site in the sun in poor, sandy soil. Make sure you sow it in its final position – it has a rather long tap root and doesn't respond well to being dug up and moved. Deadheading the flowers will help promote new buds throughout the summer. Borage also grows well in pots, but make sure you stake the plants as they have a tendency to flop when unsupported.

BREW IT
Roughly chop a small handful of fresh leaves, place them in a cup and cover

with boiling water. Leave to infuse for 5–10 minutes, then strain, serve and sip your subtly tannic tea.

HEALTH BENEFITS

Both the flowers and leaves of borage – as well as the oil from its seeds – are used extensively in herbal medicine to treat gastrointestinal disorders. Borage is also used as a treatment for colds and lung infections. In Arabic, borage is called 'The father of sweat', which alludes to the plant's diaphoretic properties.

BLEND IT

Try blending a few leaves with other herby brews and use the blue flowers as a garnish for fancy iced teas.

Cherry

(Prunus)

In his collection of acclaimed pastoral poems, A. E. Housman described the cherry as the 'loveliest of trees'. Henry VIII thought so too – on a trip to Flanders he was so captivated by its handsome visage and tasty fruits that he ordered the planting of Britain's first cherry orchard in Sittingbourne, Kent. We are also big fans, as the cherry happens to be a rather versatile caddy ally. You can make a tea from the bark, stalks and blossoms, while the fruits can be squeezed into splendid syrups for the loveliest of teas.

FORAGE IT

Search and locate cherry trees in springtime by spotting the emerging clusters of white or pink cup-shaped flowers in woodland and pasture. Make a note of the location, so you can get in quick when the fruits mature and before birds raid your intended stash. There are a few different varieties you may stumble across when out foraging: plum cherry (*Prunus cerasifera*), bird cherry (*Prunus padus*), sour cherry (*Prunus cerasus*) and wild cherry (*Prunus avium*). You may also spy varieties of ornamental cherry trees growing in parkland, but remember that foraging in local parks isn't strictly foraging – it's kind of stealing – so always seek permission first before you start bothering the bows for your tea-making experiments.

sweet and sour varieties – the sweet cherries require pollination partners in order to produce fruit, so you may need to plant a pollinating pal.

GROW IT

Planting a cherry is easy, just follow the tried-and-tested fruit tree method (see *page 93*). Cherry trees come in

BREW THE STALKS

To make cherry stalk tea, take a handful of cherries, remove the fruits then dry out the stalks, either on a

HOW TO PICKLE CHERRY BLOSSOMS TO MAKE SAKURA TEA

1 Gather 2 cups of pink blossoms in springtime, just as they are emerging.

2 Combine with 2 tsp of salt and place in the fridge for 2–3 days.

3 Press the blossoms with a paper towel to remove excess moisture, then cover with ¼ cup plum vinegar and leave to marinate for a further 3 days.

4 Drain off the vinegar and allow the blossoms to dry before storing in a jam jar packed with salt.

5 To make Sakura Tea, place 3–4 of the salted, pickled blossoms in a cup and pour over boiling water.

warm windowsill or in a dehydrator. Take a healthy pinch of dried stalks, drop them in a cup, add boiling water and leave to steep for 10 minutes. Strain then serve for a delicate, lightly tannic brew.

BREW THE FRUIT

Turn the stalkless cherries into syrups for making fruity brews like our Blackberry Frappé (see *page 172*).

BREW THE BARK

Wild cherry bark tea is supposedly good for soothing coughs. A slither of bark should be chopped and dried before adding a couple of teaspoons to a mug of boiling water. It makes for a pretty astringent woody tasting brew (unsurprisingly), so it needs to be blended with other more palatable cup buddies. Try smoothing those rough edges with a healthy dose of mint.

BREW THE BLOSSOM

The fruits of ornamental varieties such as the Japanese cherry (*Prunus serrulata*) tend to be too sharp to be used in syrups without adding industrial levels of sugar to balance out the acidity. Instead, gather their blossoms in springtime and attempt to make a salty, umami Sakura Tea (see above).

HEALTH BENEFITS

Cherry stalk tea has been used in the treatment of inflammation of the bladder. It's also deemed to be a pretty effective laxative. Go careful now...

BLEND IT

Anyone with a penchant for fruity pies knows that cherry goes well with cinnamon, so add 1 or 2 pinches to your syrup or cherry stalk tea. Loose leaf black tea also tastes great with the addition of a few drops of cherry syrup.

WARNING!

Some parts of cherries, in particular the pits (or seeds) – along with apricots, almonds, peaches and plums – contain small amounts of cyanide. Although you would conceivably have to ingest quite a lot in order for it to have an effect, all cherry-based teas should be drunk in moderation.

Liquorice

(Glycyrrhiza glabra)

The liquorice plant possesses one of the tastiest roots around with a depth of flavour few other ingredients can match. Besides its obvious similarity to aniseed it has a moreish earthy quality and so much sweetness it actually tastes juicy. And there's even more good news for wild tea brewers — it's a healthy tonic too.

GROW IT

Liquorice's dream environment is somewhere warm on the banks of a river or stream. To grow your own in the garden, give it your sunniest spot in well-draining soil — ideally one that is sandy. Seeds can be tricky to germinate and young plants are vulnerable to the cold, so protect them from frost for a few years before planting out.

Once established, and given the right conditions, the plant will develop a long tap root and rhizomes that can spread to cover a large area. To harvest, dig up the plant in late autumn and cut away the roots leaving the crown intact. You'll then need to nurture this crown through winter by storing it in compost somewhere cool and dark before planting out again in spring. If all this sounds like too much work then dried roots are readily available for culinary purposes.

BREW IT

To get the full flavours of liquorice in a tea you're better off decocting the root. Cut off a piece around 5 cm (2 in) long, split it lengthways and give it a gentle bashing with a pestle and mortar before simmering for a minimum of 10 minutes in enough boiling water for your mug plus an extra third to allow for evaporation. Chopping and grinding makes it suitable for steeping, with a pinch or two of the resulting powder adding its rich, flavoursome notes to tea blends.

HEALTH BENEFITS

Liquorice roots contain hundreds of different chemical compounds and the list of potential health benefits from these is vast. Scientists have been busily studying the root to ascertain its healing capabilities in numerous areas including skin conditions, stomach pains, cough treatments, hepatitis C and tooth decay.* Despite all this potential goodness, liquorice also contains toxins which can cause health problems if taken in excess.

BLEND IT

You'll find liquorice sneaking into lots of caffeine-free, commercially available teas, where it adds complexity to many flavour combinations. Try it with leafy brews to give them some depth of flavour and a natural sweetness.

DID YOU KNOW?

The Dutch and Norwegians love liquorice-flavoured sweets, some of which are mixed with salty-tasting ammonium chloride and are known as *salmiak*. It is an acquired taste, but one that is worth persevering with.

* *However, regularly scoffing liquorice sweets will almost certainly encourage tooth decay.*

Lemongrass

(Cymbopogon citratus)

A hero of Thai cooking, lemongrass has sweet, aromatic lemon flavours that add a freshness to food and drinks without the acidic tang of its citrussy namesake. The leaves and stalks can both be used to make tea, with the latter doubling up as a handy stirring implement.

GROW IT

Lemongrass can be a little tricky to grow away from the tropical parts of the world it favours. Nick once kept a plant alive for two years before it perished, either through lack of heat, humidity or incorrect watering. Healthy, longer-living lemongrass plants can grow into huge, grassy clumps. There are only a few of the fifty plus lemongrass varieties that are used for cooking so if you're growing your own be certain it's edible.

BREW IT

You can use the stalks (2 stalks per cup, outer layer removed and bashed to release their flavour), but you get much more value from steeping the leaves (1 tsp per cup) in a cup of boiling water for 5 minutes. Both parts can also be dried. Try lemongrass on its own or with black tea, serve hot or cold, and give it some extra zest with a lime garnish.

HEALTH BENEFITS

There are countless health claims surrounding lemongrass, from the

TURN STALKS INTO PLANTS

You can grow your own lemongrass plants from shop-bought stalks, providing they have some of the base still intact. Simply remove any loose or dry outer layers and place them in a jar of water, filled to cover the lower third of the stalks. Refresh the water every few days and eventually roots will appear. When you have a healthy nest of small roots put the stalks into a pot filled with compost (you can stick several stalks in one pot and grow as a clump) and keep indoors until established.

relief of anxiety to the prevention of infections, but we can't find much in the way of proven benefits. It features regularly in Ayurvedic health brews and is popular for medicinal teas in Brazil where it's often paired with pineapple.

BLEND IT

Lemongrass blends well with other fruity and spicy flavours such as apple, ginger and cinnamon.

Beetroot

(Beta vulgaris)

Beetroot has enjoyed a long history of culinary and medicinal use.
Evidence of beetroot cultivation can be traced back to Neolithic times,
while the Ancient Greeks were avid growers (although they ate the leaves,
not the roots). The Romans were especially fond of beetroot, and the plant
features heavily in the Apicius manuscript. After a hard day marching
around in uncomfortable sandals, they would often cheer themselves with
a carafe or two of wine and a nice beetroot salad. The Romans never really
took to tea drinking, but we think they missed a trick – when comes to
making tasty, veg-based beverages, this bulbous, ruddy root is hard to beet.

GROW IT

Beetroot is one of the easiest veg to
grow, making it a firm favourite on
our allotment. It prefers to grow in
well-drained soil and will thrive in
fertile conditions, so if you can, dig
in some well-rotted manure prior
to planting. Harvest beetroot when
the roots are the size of golf balls, as
that's when they are at their most
flavoursome.

BREW IT

Beetroot makes for a fine brew, hot
or iced. It's a good idea to wear gloves
during preparation as this ruddy-hued
root will stain your hands crimson,
making it look like you've been party
to some kind of gruesome crime.*

For a hot, tasty chai, grate ½ a
beetroot into a cup, then add a couple
of pinches of grated ginger. Top up the
cup with boiling water, cover it with
a saucer and allow to steep for 10–15
minutes. To serve, add a squeeze of
lemon juice and 1 tsp of honey.

For an iced beetroot tea, follow
the instructions above, but allow it to
cool completely before straining and
pouring over ice. Add a couple of sprigs
of mint for a fresh summer flourish.

HEALTH BENEFITS

Studies have shown that eating
beetroot can significantly lower
blood pressure and fight heart disease.
It is also believed to increase libido,
working in a similar way to Viagra by
increasing nitric oxide levels in the
body and increasing blood flow to your
nether regions.

BLEND IT

Besides making a crimson-coloured
chai (see above), dried beetroot can be
used in healthy tonics and pairs well
with sweet apple (see Harvest Brew
page 128).

DID YOU KNOW?

Garlic breath can be
nullified by a glass
of beetroot juice.
We've yet to come
across a vegetable
that nullifies
beetroot breath.

* *If you were unimpressed
by the results of our
lemon tea recipes on
page 88, you could
always use them as
handwash – lemon juice
can help remove beetroot
stains from hands.*

Best of
the Rest

In this section we feature even more of
our favourite ingredients, chosen for
their brewing brilliance or because of
the teatime tales they can tell...

ACORNS

The small nuts from the mighty oak can be roasted to make coffee (see *page 169*).

ANISE

The seeds of this Mediterranean plant are used in many sweets and boozes, including ouzo, absinthe, arak, sambuca and pastis. They also impart a sweet liquorice-like flavour to tea blends. Lightly crush a teaspoonfull before adding to hot water. In Holland, an aniseed-flavoured, milky brew called *anijsmelk* is very popular. Simply add 1 tsp of aniseed to a mug of milk and heat in a pan. When it reaches boiling point, turn down the heat and simmer for 5 minutes. Strain into a mug and stir in 2 tsp of honey for sweetness.

ANISE HYSSOP

This perennial herb is neither anise nor hyssop. However, it does have a minty taste similar to hyssop with a sprinkling of anise flavour and as such is great to grow for teas.

BANANA

There has been a recent trend for boiling banana peel to make a pre-bed tea that can supposedly help you sleep. It's not for us and, as bananas receive a lot of chemical spraying, anyone keen on trying it should make sure their fruit is organic. Dried bananas yield little flavour when infused yet 3–4 crushed slices in a cup makes a surprisingly enjoyable drink, with just a whisper of banana sweetness emerging.

BARLEY

This cereal crop is grown for beer, whisky and Roasted Barley Tea (see *page 144*).

BASIL

Roughly 5 medium-sized fresh sweet basil leaves (*Ocimum basilicum*) make a tea with a tasty tingle; the herb also complements some fruity brews. Even better is lemon basil (*Ocimum basilicum* var. *citriodorum*), which has the added benefit of punchy lemony notes.

BERGAMOT

A citrus fruit that's a bit like a sour orange and is used to flavour Earl Grey tea.

BLACK PEPPER

A pinch of pepper does wonders for warming up a cup of tea and is very useful in spiced beverages.

BURDOCK

In the UK, we're familiar with the use of burdock as a double act with dandelion in a soft drink, and the two also used to team up in ancient meads and beers. Burdock's seeds have hooks, which easily attach to clothes and have been claimed to be the inspiration for the invention of Velcro, but it's the unusual mild, earthy flavour of the roots that are responsible for the plant's use in cooking and tea making.

BAMBOO

While the shoots of bamboo are commonly used in Chinese cooking, it's the young leaves of some varieties that are used for tea. Apparently they're rich in silica, which is claimed to promote hair growth, and as we've never seen a bald panda, who are we to disagree.

BLUEBERRY / BILBERRY

Both leaves and berries are suitable for tea making, with the latter making a colourful addition to fruity blends. If you can't find them in the wild, then grow them at home in acidic soil – ours are confined to pots and in autumn we race the birds to pick them. Their smooth skins are good at holding in the juice, so cut them in half for speedier drying. Confusingly, 'blueberry tea' is also the name of a cocktail that doesn't contain blueberries.

CARAWAY

Also known as Persian cumin and meridian fennel, these seeds are a common flavouring in rye bread. They have a milder aniseed flavour than fennel and are earthier, with a slight peppery warmth.

CARROT

Russians like a wild tea – they have been known to blend carrot tops with black tea and sometimes used dried carrots as a tea substitute during World War II.

CARDAMOM

The seed pods from two types of cardamom are used as a spice – green cardamom, which comes from the Indian plant species *Elettaria cardomomum*, and the Himalyan black cardamom, which comes from *Amomum subulatum*. The green pods are most commonly used in teas and are an essential ingredient of traditional masala chais (see *page 130*).

CASSAVA

A rooty crop from which tapioca is extracted (see Bubble Tea on *page 162*).

CATNIP

Also known as 'cat crack'. This member of the mint family makes a decent, minty-tasting tea with a slight hint of citrus. Use 1–2 tsp of dried flowers per cup. Cat owning home-workers should avoid perching a glass of catnip tea beside their laptop for obvious reasons.

CHICORY

The roasted roots make a good coffee substitute (see *page 169*).

CHILLI

Choose a variety that's easy to grow in your garden, greenhouse or on the windowsill and use it fresh or dried to add a kick to hot drinks like chai (see *page 130*).

CINNAMON

The inner bark of the cinnamon tree plays a supporting role in several of our teas, delivering a warming, feel-good presence to every nostril its aroma meets. It is the essence of the festive season and can work its magic on just about any tea going. We prefer to use sticks rather than ground powder, which can be dropped into decoctions whole or crumbled into blends. For a solo cinnamon tea, try simmering 1 stick in a mug's worth of water for 5 minutes.

CLEAVERS

The small round seeds that have a habit of sticking to your clothes can be roasted for an excellent alternative to coffee (see *page 169*).

CLOVES

These spicy little sticks are actually dried flower buds from the Indonesian clove tree. They're used in sweet and savoury dishes and are often in demand at Christmas when they're added to all sorts of mulled beverages, including winter-warming teas.

COCONUT

Coconut flavouring often appears in commercial teas, chocolates, coffee blends and syrups, but we use it most as a milk substitute.

COMMON MALLOW

We sowed and nurtured some common mallow plants (*Mallow sylvestris*) as their leaves and flowers were reputed to make a decent, healthy tea. The results were revolting, so we won't bother again.

CORNFLOWER

Cornflower's bright blue petals are often added to tea blends, notably Earl Grey, mainly to liven their appearance with a touch of colour.

CRANBERRY

These tart little berries work as well in teas as they do in festive

Above from top: lemon basil, sweet woodruff.

sauces. They are best in blends that feature sweeter fruits, with orange providing a common partner. Like blueberries, they're a heathland plant that requires acidic soil – home-growers can also benefit from picking leaves for tea making.

CUCUMBER

A member of the Cucurbitaceae family, which also includes melons, squashes and pumpkins, the cucumber is loved for its cooling character, making it popular for iced teas (see *page 158*).

EPAZOTE

This native of Central America and Mexico is a member of the goosefoot family and is so revered for its tea that it's also known as Jesuit's tea and Mexican tea. It also goes by the name stink weed and has the translated name skunk sweat because it emits an aroma like a filthy lorry leaking fuel. We read that it tastes better than it smells, but it doesn't. We grow a plant in a container as one of the chemicals responsible for the stench (ascaridole) can also inhibit the growth of neighbouring plants. It has been used to kill parasites in humans and pets, and Mexicans reckon it can help reduce bloating and any resulting flatulence, so often serve it with beans – although go easy because it's toxic and could induce vomiting or far worse.

FEVERFEW

Drinking feverfew tea was once believed to give the drinker fewer fevers but now its most common use is in preventing migraines. It's a member of the daisy family and has very strongly scented leaves not dissimilar in flavour to sage. Steep 3 leaves (fresh or dried) in a cup full of hot water for 2–3 minutes for a delicately soothing brew.

GRASS CLIPPINGS

Nope.

GROUND IVY

Low-lying *Glechoma hederacea* is a member of the mint family and can be found at the edges of fields and parks or creeping into the corners of unweeded gardens. It has dainty blue flowers and its green leaves can become tinged with purple, depending on the nutritional content of the soil it roots in. Use 6–8 fresh leaves picked in spring (or 1 tsp of dried leaves) for a tea that has a sage-like herbiness with a minty tingle and peppery bitterness. These flavours make it a useful hop substitute for beer, hence its alternative name – alehoof. It's not to everyone's taste, but we like it and think it works well in mint and aniseed blends.

HIMALAYAN BALSAM

In order to help eradicate this invasive riverbank menace, we'd love to be able to say that Himalayan balsam makes a lovely brew. We can't. The best we can suggest is that you can freeze its (admittedly handsome) flowers into ice cubes and then float them in a nice iced tea (see *pages 154* and *158*).

JASMINE

The blossoms of the common jasmine (*Jasminum officinale*), or the national flower of the Philippines (*Jasminum sambac*), are blended with other teas, most commonly green, to produce the popular aromatic jasmine tea. The tea is often sold as 'pearls' – rolled up green tea leaves that have been infused with jasmine's fragrance.

LIME

Lime's main function in Western drinks is as a garnishing alternative to lemon. We think it deserves more attention than that and happily use it in cold teas for some sour fruitiness (see Tropical Hibiscus Sun Tea, *page 149*).

In Arabian countries, it takes even more of the limelight (pun intended) and a popular tea is made from the dried fruits (commonly called *limu Omani* because the drying method originated in Oman). You'll need 1 lime per cup (add another half for a large mug) broken into chunks and simmered in a cup's worth of water for 5 minutes before serving and sweetening to taste.

MARSHMALLOW

The roots from this wild perennial were the original flavouring ingredient for the sweet favoured by amateur bonfire chefs. They also crop up in tea blends that promote relaxation and calmness.

MUGWORT

This wild cousin to wormwood can be used as an alternative to its more bitter relative.

OLIVE LEAF

Dried olive leaves make a tea that is rich in vitamins and antioxidants. It can take a while for the flavours to fully seep out, so steep for as long as you can. You'll be rewarded with a very silky, mellow brew that has a unique flavour verging on fishiness, but try not to let that put you off as it's better than it sounds.

ORANGE

This much enjoyed citrus fruit can be useful to add some sweet juicy flavours to blends and is a winning choice for chocolatey drinks (see *page 128*).

PELARGONIUM

Confusingly, pelargoniums are often called geraniums, which is the name of another plant group and not something you want to use in your beverages. To mark their difference they're sometimes known as scented geraniums on account of their strong aromas.

To be sure you're dealing with something both edible and tasty, seek out the daintily pink-flowered variety 'Attar of Roses', which has a heady fragrance of Turkish delight that is much admired by perfumers and dessert makers. Or try 'Orange Fizz', which has pink and purple flowers and an outrageously zesty orange flavour.

The best way to get these flavours into a tea, coffee, cake or pastry is by making a scented sugar from pelargonium leaves. Finely chop 3 leaves, mix them into 100 g (3½ oz) of caster sugar and seal in a jar for 24 hours before opening.

PUZZLEWEED

Alas, there is no such plant as the puzzleweed. It is here simply to make sure that everyone reading this is paying attention.

RED CLOVER

Red clover can be found dotted around fields in early summer, nodding its fluffy pink heads among the swathes of green grass. These flowers make a pleasant cup of tea and you only need 4–5 fresh heads per mug. The tea is very delicate and, as such, hard to describe – we're going with a faintly sweet melon-ish aroma and a dry, hay-like flavour. And if you're hoping you'll be sipping on a pink or red brew then you're out of luck – the hot water makes it turn a vivid lime green.

RHUBARB

This vegetable thinks it's a fruit. It combines excellently with ginger (see *page 167* for more).

ROOIBOS

Rooibos (or red bush) is a rugged, broom-like plant that grows in the Cederberg region of South Africa. Its needle-shaped leaves are oxidized and made into a caffeine-free tea which has a sweet, nutty taste. When asking for it in posh tea houses, you should pronounce it 'roy-boss' to demonstrate your exemplary tea knowledge thanks to reading this book.

Left: anise, caraway, star anise.

Opposite, clockwise from top left: ground ivy, cornflower, epazote, feverfew, pelargonium.

STAR ANISE

A popular Chinese spice that tastes like its namesake, anise, and looks like a star. See *page 151* for its star brewing qualities.

STEVIA

This sweet-leaved Brazilian native is seen as a miracle sugar replacement by some and a mysterious evil by others – it has even been banned in some countries. We've made several unsuccessful attempts to grow it from seed (germination is tricky), so bought an established plant instead. The leaves should be picked before flowering and, although we've heard that some plants fail to deliver sweetness, ours has it in great abundance.

SWEET WOODRUFF

Also known as *Waldmeister* and wild baby's breath, this ground-hugging herb can be spotted growing in gardens and in dappled woodland shade. Dry out the leaves and steep them in hot water for a floral brew that smells like freshly mown hay – the longer you steep, the more fragrant your tea will be. Flick over to *page 166* for our woodruff syrup recipe.

THYME

This herb is disappointing in the tea-making department, with an oily flavour that doesn't suit hot drinks. However, it is worth growing for soups and stews, and so you can make 'tea thyme' jokes (not that we would stoop so low).

TULSI

Looks a bit like basil, tastes a bit like basil, makes a tea a bit like basil and is also called holy basil. But it's a different plant to the more well-known culinary basil. We've found it a bit less reliable to grow than sweet basil but if you want to add some colour to your greenhouse then a purple-leaved variety is worth a go.

TURMERIC

Turmeric root is a common favourite of Asian curries and has recently been transformed into a star drinks ingredient, lending its glorious golden hue to whatever dish it's added to. The turmeric plant is a relative of ginger and prefers to grow in the hot and wet parts of India and Asia. Simmer 1–2 tsp in water to make a tea or turn to *page 142* for our version of the popular turmeric latté.

VALERIAN

The roots of common valerian (*Valeriana officinalis*, not to be confused with other plants with the valerian moniker) have long been used as a tea for insomniacs, and it cuddles up with other sleepy ingredients in Sue's Hop to Bed brew (see *page 126*). In medieval times, the plants were tucked into Swedish grooms' wedding clothes to see off jealous elves.

WORMWOOD

This attractive, silvery-green-leafed perennial is a good looker in flower borders and is sometimes known as green ginger, madder wort or bitter hellion. The leaves of the variety *Artemisia absinthium* have a powerfully bitter flavour and are used in absinthe, vermouth and herbal liqueurs. Thujone is present in the leaves and is said to be one of the chemicals responsible for absinthe's notoriety as a mind-bending booze. Wormwood is also used as a medicinal tea, most commonly to treat intestinal problems, and is mixed with green tea in Morocco as an alternative to mint.

Blends

To be a true wild tea master, you've got to blend. Mixing together different dried tea ingredients allows you to create a whole range of flavour combinations that you can store and dip into for an instant brew whenever the mood strikes.

PERFECT PARTNERS

To set you on the path to blending brilliance here are some of our favourite double acts. Try playing around with the proportions of each ingredient to get a feel for how the flavours work in combination with each other and, if you're feeling in an experimental mood, introduce a third flavour to build a more uniquely complex blend.

MINT AND LEMON

You could pair mint or lemon with just about any other ingredient in this book and strike a winning combination, so it's no surprise that they relish each other's company. We like our mint with a hint of lemon and, for all the more complicated blends and recipes in this book, it's a tea that is very hard to beat.

Serve: 2 tsp per cup
3 parts dried mint leaves
1 part dried lemon peel

RHUBARB AND GINGER

Rhubarb is one of many foods that claims to be ginger's best friend. There's something about ginger's zingy warmth that makes the tart-flavoured pink sticks from our unruly allotment-dwelling rhubarb seem faintly exotic. Before drying rhubarb, slice it into pencil-thick strips and it will soon shrivel into string, making it easy to break into your tea blend. Garnish with an orange wheel to bring out the vegetable's fruitier side.

Serve: 1 tsp per cup
1 part dried ginger
1 part dried rhubarb
1 orange wheel, to garnish (optional)

APPLE AND CINNAMON

Baked apples are always improved by a pinch of cinnamon, and you can recreate that comforting autumnal combination in tea form.

Serve: 2 tsp per cup
3 parts dried apple
2 parts cinnamon stick

Crumble a cinnamon stick with small chunks of dried apple and infuse for a good 10 minutes (or simmer in a pan if you don't mind the extra washing up). Apple is naturally sweet, but if you crave more sweetness add some brown sugar.

A NOTE ON QUANTITIES

The quantities in this section are based on the volume of dried ingredients when crumbled, chopped or ground. We've measured them as proportional 'parts' so you can decide on your own quantities. For example, if you're making an initial small experimental batch then make each 'part' a teaspoon; for larger batches each part can be measured out in a larger volume. For each of these blends, infuse in hot water for 5 minutes unless otherwise stated.

THREE OF A KIND

When coming up with combinations of three or more ingredients, it can help to narrow down the choice by thinking of things that naturally go together. This could be anything from ingredients that have a similar flavour, to plants that share the same season, or even those that grow together. Here we've taken inspiration from our own garden, a trip to the coast and the tea-friendly flavours of lemon...

WILD GARDEN TEA

Being lazy gardeners, we'll use any excuse to avoid the hard labour of weeding, so are grateful that some of the plants that have bullied their way into our gardens make excellent teas. This blend is a combination of three favourite wild plants that others consider weeds – so dodge the digging, hang up your hoes and get to work on this wholesome brew instead.

Serve: 2 tsp per cup
5 parts dried dandelion flowers
3 parts dried nettle leaves
3 parts dried yarrow leaves

THREE WAYS WITH LEMON

Have you noticed how fancy modern chefs like to show off their range of culinary skills by serving up the same ingredient in three different ways? This is our liquid antidote to such cheffy nonsense – a tea made with three ingredients that all taste of lemon. To compliment the zesty lemon of the actual fruit, we've introduced the sherbet flavours of lemon verbena and the calming herbal notes of lemon balm. Three lemons, one great tea.

Serve: 1 tsp per cup
2 parts dried lemon verbena leaves
1 part dried lemon balm leaves
1 part dried lemon peel

COASTAL CUPPA

This caramel-hued, sweet-tasting brew was inspired by plants foraged on the Cornish coastal cliffs of St Ives. We would suggest dunking in a Cornish Fairing biscuit to provide a bonus ginger hit. To get a bracing taste of the Atlantic, add a sprinkle of bladder wrack (if you dare).

Serve: 1 tsp per cup
2 parts dried nettle leaves
1 part dried meadowsweet flowers
2 parts dried gorse flowers

TEA TWISTS

These three blends are based on some of the most popular teas from around the world, each with a wild tea twist to make them an instant homemade success.

CHINA TEA WITH ROSE

Rose Congou tea (or China rose tea) is an ancient blend that is made by layering rose petals with tea leaves during their oxidization process. This allows a floral fragrance to permeate the tea. For a short-cut version, you can simply mix dried rose petals with China black tea (you can, of course, use any black tea, but we think this works well with the mellow flavours of Keemum). Leave for at least a couple of days to give the floral flavours time to infuse.

For a caffeine-free alternative, try substituting the black tea with another dried leaf – we've found the combination of rose and nettle is a winner.

Serve: 1 tsp per cup
2 parts China black tea
1 part dried rose petals

THRIFTY SHADES OF (EARL) GREY

The popular aromatic Earl Grey is black tea that has been flavoured with bergamot oil. Anyone who grows bee balm (*Monarda didyma*) can take advantage of its bergamot-esque flavour and blend it with black tea for a cheap home-made version. It's not a totally accurate replica, but there are enough similar shades to make it an enjoyable alternative for Earl Grey fans.

Serve: 1 tsp per cup
2 parts black tea
1 part dried *Monarda didyma* leaves

Crush the dried *Monarda didyma* leaves, combine with the black tea and give them a couple of days infusion time before using. Earl Grey itself is often combined with dried citrus peel and cornflower petals, so try using either to add a bit of colour to your own grey blend.

CHEAT'S MOROCCAN MINT TEA

A proper Moroccan mint tea should be made precisely and with fresh mint (see page 137) but this dried version still tastes great and is well worth making in a big batch to keep in your dried tea collection.

Serve: 1 tsp per cup
3 parts green tea
2 parts dried mint leaves

Simply mix the green tea with crushed, dried mint leaves and use 1 tsp per cup. To increase authenticity, you can pile sugar into your cup, but we prefer it without. Moroccans are also known to add other ingredients to their mint teas including lemon verbena, star anise, saffron and wormwood,* so try experimenting with some of these flavours too.

* *Wormwood comes with a warning: it is intensely bitter, so only a touch is required.*

DAY AND NIGHT

Imagine having the same meal for breakfast, lunch and supper. And imagine not changing that meal the next day, or the next — even if you wake feeling a little groggy or are eager to wind down for an early night. Just as we appreciate some timely order to our eating habits, we like to vary our tea-drinking accordingly. Here, then, are three teas to see you safely through the day.

MORNING AFTER THE NIGHT BEFORE TEA

Everyone swears by their own hangover cure, but there has been very little scientific research or indeed evidence to support their effectiveness. The hazardous nature of our job has led us to try most of them over the years, and we think this tea blend is as good as any. Borage and turmeric will help detoxify your polluted body, peppermint will help ease your sour stomach and freshen your stale, beery breath.

Serve: 1 tsp per cup
1 part borage leaves (fresh or dried)
1 part turmeric
3 parts dried peppermint leaves

AFTER-DINNER TEA

Over done it on the apple crumble? Then this tea will aid digestion and improve your stomach's ills. In India, fennel seeds are eaten as an alternative to after-dinner mints, so mint and fennel make an obvious combination, while ginger is good at soothing upset stomachs and fighting indigestion. Together, their powerful flavour will also make you feel fresh and ready to face the rest of the day.

Serve: 2 tsp per cup
1 part dried mint leaves
1 part fennel seeds
1 part dried ginger pieces, or ground ginger

SUE'S 'HOP TO BED' TEA

One of our go-to experts on the wellbeing benefits of natural ingredients is Sue Mullet, who puts her knowledge to good use by producing some amazing elixirs at Bath Botanical Gin Distillery and Herbal Apothecary. She also blends teas, with one of her most popular being this concoction, which is designed to be taken before heading off to bed – the hops, valerian, lavender and lime flower all have calming properties that will set you in the right mood for sleep. We like it so much that we nicked the recipe from under Sue's nose while she was taking a nap...

Serve: 1 tsp per cup
3 parts dried hops
1 part valerian roots
1 part dried lime flowers
1 part dried lavender flowers

SPRING AND SUMMER BLENDS

Spring and summer see us working at our hardest in the garden: weeding and sowing, digging and hoeing, cutting and mowing, but mostly puffing and blowing (and cursing) trying to get the barbecue to work properly. These teas provide some light refreshment from the seasonal stresses and strains.

SUMMER FLOWER TEA

This blend combines some of our favourite floral ingredients, each readily available from our gardens during the summer months. Elderflower and marigold are the more delicate constituents, so they each have double quantities; the chamomile adds a unique fruity fragrance and the hint of lavender provides a subtle, soothing summer tingle at the finish. For an alternative flower arrangement, you could try switching the chamomile with rose petals.

Serve: 2 tsp per cup
2 parts dried elderflowers
2 parts dried marigolds
1 part dried lavender flowers
1 part dried chamomile flowers

SPRING GREEN LEAF TEA

There is a time in spring, when the landscape is cloaked in every shade of green imaginable and garden growth goes into overdrive. For the first time in the year, we have to put in a hard stint of work to keep on top of things. This is a tea for such moments of hard graft – an invigorating, leafy brew that refreshes the system like a drop of oil in a squeaky pair of secateurs. It's equally good served hot or ice cold with a slice of lemon.

Serve: 2 tsp per cup	
2 parts dried lemon balm leaves	2 parts dried blackberry leaves
1 part dried mint leaves	1 part dried rosemary leaves

THE THIRSTY GARDENER TEA

For us, summer arrives when the first spruce and pine tips emerge, and ends when our allotment hops ripen. This tea is one of our most refreshing summer drinks, slaking our thirst and acting as a foil for spruce tips, hops, or other aromatic additions such as the year-round rosemary, which can be freshly plucked and dunked into the brew. The hoppy recipe also provided the inspiration for our tea-flavoured beer, expertly brewed by St Austell Brewery (see *page 150*).

Serve: 1 tsp per cup	**Optional**
1 part dried lemon verbena leaves	2 fresh hops/5 spruce or pine tips/a sprig of rosemary per cup
1 part green tea	

AUTUMN AND WINTER BLENDS

Hot drinks come into their own during the colder months of the year and any winter chills can be banished further with the introduction of some warming spice. These blends are among the cosiest brews you can find, providing some rich seasonal flavours that will help defend you against the elements.

SPICED ORANGE HOT CHOCOLATE MIX

There are times during long, dark evenings when the comfort of warming spice isn't enough and the extra satisfaction of indulgence is required. Time to crack open the cocoa. This blend will bring extra cheer to your hot chocolate with its tickling of orange and spice.

Blend
1 part dried orange peel
1 part cinnamon stick, crumbled
1 part dried ginger pieces or ground ginger
1 part dried bay leaf

Hot chocolate
1⅓ cups of milk
2 tbsp cocoa powder
2 tsp spiced orange hot chocolate mix
2 tsp sugar

To make, simply add 1⅓ cups of milk to a pan (the extra is to allow for evaporation) and steadily bring to a boil. Take the milk off the heat and whisk in the cocoa powder, then add the spices and sugar. Return to the heat and gently simmer for 5–10 minutes, stirring as you go. Strain and serve.

HARVEST BREW

Autumn is a busy time for wild tea makers – digging roots from the allotment, plucking fruit from trees and roaming the hedgerows for forageable goods – and this ruddy brew is a reward for those harvesting efforts.

Serve: 2 tsp per cup
2 parts dried apple
1 part dried beetroot
1 part dried rosehips
1 part dried ginger pieces or ground ginger

Chop or grind the sweet apple, earthy beetroot, fruity rosehips and spicy ginger. Combine and steep in a cup of hot water for at least 5 minutes before basking in a healthy harvest glow.

A FESTIVE BREW

If you're a fan of the festive flavours that go into a mulled wine but fancy something free from booze, then this is the brew for you.

Serve: 2 tsp per cup
3 parts dried blackcurrant leaves
3 parts dried hibiscus flowers
2 parts dried rosehips
2 parts cinnamon stick, crumbled
1 part liquorice root
1 part dried ginger pieces or ground ginger

Blend the ingredients and steep for 10 minutes in a cup of boiling water then breathe in its heady aroma and sup. On its own it makes a soothing tea, but for an extra kick try adding a pinch of chilli powder to each cup.

HEALTHY BREWS

Although some of the health claims surrounding our tea ingredients are wilder than the back of Rich's allotment, there is evidence that many of them can do some good. These teas have been created with their health and wellbeing properties in mind.

NEW MUM'S (AND OLD DAD'S) TEA

One of the biggest boom areas for healthy teas is blends designed for new mums. Nettle and fennel are often a feature of these concoctions as they can aid the production of breast milk, while a pinch of chamomile can help to keep mum calm during times of tiny tantrums. Seeing as we're a couple of old dads we cannot personally vouch for this tea's effectiveness, but drink it anyway because it tastes great.

Serve: 2 tsp per cup
2 parts dried nettle leaves
2 parts fennel seeds
1 part dried chamomile flowers

COLD-BUSTING TEA

It may be true that there's no cure for the common cold, but you can certainly perk yourself up with a healthy dose of vitamins. These ingredients provide an alphabet soup of vitamin goodness, with C common to them all.

Serve: 3 tsp per cup
2 parts dried rosehips
2 parts dried elderberries
2 parts dried echinacea leaves
1 part dried lemon peel

Steep for 10 minutes (or simmer in water to extract even more flavour) in a cup of hot water and sup slowly when the cold bug is next doing the rounds.

ENERGY TEA

Can a cup of tea really give you energy? If any tea can, then it's this one. It combines the eye-widening stimulants of yerba mate with the all-round goodness of liquorice, and an equal measure of mint for some extra flavour.

Serve: 2 tsp per cup
1 part dried yerba mate leaves
1 part liquorice root
1 part dried mint leaves

Steep in a cup of hot water for at least 5 minutes before drinking – it may not give you enough energy to run a marathon, but it will certainly snap you out of a work-time slumber.

CHAI

There is an infinite array of masala chais you could make, but there are essentially two ways to make them: with care, love and fresh ingredients (see *page 138*) or with pre-made, dried blends for people with less time on their hands (read on).

USING THE BLENDS

For each of these blends you'll need 3 tsp per cup and you can make them with milk, water or a combination of both. For speedy chais, simply steep the ingredients in just-boiled liquid for a minimum of 5 minutes; for a fuller flavour, simmer them in a pan for 10 minutes. Sweeten to taste.

BASIC GINGER CHAI

If you were to take a survey of the five key ingredients for masala chai, this selection might well come out on top. It's certainly a good place to start before experimenting with your own blends. We like a touch of black pepper for an extra kick, but add no more than a quarter part per batch or a pinch per cup.

Serve: 3 tsp per cup
3 parts black tea
2 parts dried ginger pieces or
  ground ginger
2 parts green cardamom pods
1 part cinnamon stick
1 part fennel seeds

Chop, grind or bash all the ingredients before mixing. Add a grind of pepper if you want a fiery kick.

NICK'S ROSE GARDEN CHAI

For this chai Nick has delved into the garden for three ingredients to infuse with the more exotic spices. Rose petals add fragrance to complement the cardamom; fennel seeds give the tea some earthy, aniseedy depth; and the firey ginger has been dropped in place of the softer spice of bay leaf.

Serve: 3 tsp per cup
3 parts black tea
1 part dried rose petals
1 part cinnamon stick, crumbled
1 part fennel seeds
2 parts dried bay leaves
2 parts cardamom pods

RICH'S CHILLI CHOCCY CHAI

If he was being honest, Rich came up with the name before the recipe but, luckily, this blend turned out to be a winner. It's a fine chai to sup on winter evenings – the chilli will warm your cockles while the chocolate addition adds a luxurious texture.

Serve: 3 tsp per cup
3 parts black tea
2 parts green cardamom pods
1 part cinnamon stick, crumbled
½ part dried chilli
1 part dried ginger pieces or
  ground ginger
2 parts good-quality dark
  chocolate, chopped

Combine all the ingredients apart from the chocolate, which you should add to each cup before serving. Serve it with a swirl of cream and be a super chai guy.

Special Teas, Coffees and other Concoctions

In this section we feature some of our favourite special brews that take a little more effort than simply dunking an ingredient in hot water. We've been fermenting, roasting, cooling and mixing to produce some amazing drinks from around the world, each of them easy to make in your own home. So clear some space in the kitchen and let's brew.

Yerba Mate

Yerba mate is a smoky-tasting, antioxidant-packed brew made from the stalks and leaves of *Ilex paraguariensis*, a species of holly native to the subtropical rainforests of Argentina, Brazil and Paraguay. The beverage was first imbibed by the indigenous Guaraní and Tupi communities, with its popularity spreading across the continent through the teachings of travelling Jesuit missionaries. More recently, the drink was brought to the attention of a worldwide audience of armchair dwellers during the 2018 FIFA World Cup, when many of the South American footballing stars could be spotted disembarking their team buses clutching distinctive yerba mate gourds. Supping yerba mate in social groups is common practice in South America. To make like a pro, grab a gourd, load it with leaves and share with your yerba mate mates.

GROW IT

Ilex paraguariensis' penchant for subtropical climes confines it to South America, where this broadleaf, evergreen shrub can grow to heights of 18 m (50 ft). In order to prepare it for tea-making purposes, the leaves and stalks are cut from the mature plant and are heated to halt the oxidization process. The plant parts are then dried and stored for up to a year to help intensify flavours before heading gourd-ward and made into tea.

DRINK IT

You can make your yerba mate in a mug, but the delivery system of choice is the calabash gourd paired with a bombilla; a stainless steel straw with a perforated basket at its base to prevent the leaves entering your mouth and spoiling your herbal hit. The gourd is half-filled with leaves before adding hot (not boiling) water. Yerba mate doesn't stew like a traditional black leaf tea, so the drinking vessel can be topped up with water regularly with the leaves left to infuse several times before discarding.

MIX IT

Utilize the smoky flavours of yerba mate to make some magical mixes of your own.

Minty Yerba Mate

Combine dried garden mint with equal measures of yerba mate for a minty mix that smells a bit like menthol cigarettes (but is considerably healthier to consume).

Yerba Mate Buoy

A smoky, seaside-inspired combination. Make a mix of 2 parts yerba mate, 1 part gorse, 1 part chopped, dried rosehips and a tiny sprinkle of dried seaweed.

Jolly Holly

Step into Christmas with this festive fireside blend: 2 parts yerba mate, 1 part ginger, a curl of dried orange peel and a dash of cinnamon.

For a yerba mate energy tea packed with pick-me-up-ability, turn to *page 129*.

GROW YOUR OWN YERBA CUP

Yerba mate is traditionally served in a
hollowed-out calabash (*Lagenaria siceraria*),
also known as the bird house or bottle gourd.
The calabash grows best in warm climates,
but we've had success growing ours here in
the UK in a sheltered, south-facing garden.

HOW TO GROW

1 Sow the seeds indoors from March onwards
into individual containers. Push the seed
edge-down to help prevent rot, then cover
with a layer of vermiculite or compost.

2 Calabash, like most cucurbits, outgrow their
pots rather quickly, so pot them on before
they become root bound.

3 Move your calabashes into a cold frame
or open ground from April onwards.
Calabashes are best grown on a sunny site,
in a rich soil that has had plenty of organic
matter added. If you have the time and
inclination, prep your preferred site
before planting.

4 Calabashes love to climb – the plant will
shoot out telephone cord tendrils that will
latch onto anything for support –
so if possible grow them up and over a trellis
to allow the fruits to dangle freely. Allowing
them to ramble across the ground is fine
too, but calabashes resting on the earth
tend to grow misshapen and you may well
lose that glorious bowling pin profile.

5 Water regularly throughout the season.
Poking a cane into the soil where the taproot
lies will help you to water where the plant
needs it the most. Better still, cut the base

off a plastic bottle and slide it – neck end
first – through the cane. Push the neck into
the soil and use it as a funnel for maximum
watering efficiency.

HOW TO DRY

When fully mature, chop the gourd from its
stem and leave somewhere cool that has good
air circulation. The drying process will take a
fair few months, so be patient. Once dry, lop
off the top where the neck begins to widen into
the base. Give it a light sanding with a fine
grade sandpaper and give the outer skin a coat
or two of varnish to protect your new drinking
vessel from yerba mate spillage.

Moroccan Mint Tea

Sticking a handful of leaves in a mug of boiling water makes an excellent mint tea, but for maximum minty pleasures, make like a Moroccan. It's a ritualistic process and everyone who makes it has their own theory on how it should be done. This is the version Nick pinched from a French teamaker, Mario, at a riad in Marrakesh, who claimed it was by far the best method – and we have no reason to doubt him.

Makes: 1 teapot
2 tbsp green tea
1 large handful of
    fresh mint leaves
2 tbsp sugar

MORE THAN MINT

Although mint is the most popular, Moroccans use a variety of herbs in their teas. Experiment with variations of this recipe using sage, lemon balm, lemon verbena or whatever else takes your fancy.

1 First rinse out and warm the teapot with some boiling water.

2 Put the green tea into the pot. Ideally you want dried loose leaves (Moroccans prefer a version called Chinese gunpowder green tea) but you can get away with a few tea bags if you're desperate (meaning you can probably skip the next two instructions – just don't tell Mario).

3 Fill a heatproof glass with boiling water and pour this onto the tea, letting it stand for around a minute before giving the teapot a gentle swish and pouring the infused liquid back into the glass. This is good stuff and is known as 'the soul of the tea'.

4 Now you need to wash the green tea that's left in the teapot to get rid of some bad stuff (bitter flavours). Pour another glass of boiling water into the teapot, let it stand for a 2–3 minutes, swish, then pour the liquid away.

5 Grab a large handful of fresh mint (or two if you have tiny hands) and stuff it into the teapot along with the 'soul of the tea' from step 3 and the sugar. While 2 tbsp is a lot of sugar by our standards, many Moroccans will add more than three times that amount, so feel free to adjust to your own personal tastes. Teabag cheats should add their green tea now.

6 If you have a teapot that is heated on the hob then you can fill it up with water and bring it to a gentle boil before serving. Alternatively, fill it to the brim with freshly boiled water.

7 At this point we would usually reach for a spoon and stir the tea, but if you want to impress your pals with your tea-making nous then stir it the traditional way by pouring out a glass and immediately pouring it back into the teapot. Mario repeated this five times.

8 At long last, your tea is now ready to serve. For a final flourish of frothy authenticity, hold the spout high above the glass and pour.

Masala Chai

Masala Chai is the spiced tea that is served everywhere from chaiwala stalls on bustling Indian roadsides to restaurants, bars and cafés throughout the world. This is a basic recipe that centres on the essential ingredient of all good masala chais: cardamom. Add a few complementary spices to the fragrant green pods and simmer yourself a simple spicy treat.

Makes: 1 large mug
4 green cardamom pods
½ cinnamon stick
   (5 cm/2 in in length)
2 cloves
250 ml (9 fl oz) water
250 ml (9 fl oz) milk
2 tsp (or 2 teabags)
   black tea
Sugar, to taste

1 Gently bash the cardamom pods using a pestle and mortar until they are cracked and bruised, then put them in a pan with the cinnamon, cloves and water.

2 Bring to the boil then turn the heat down, fit a lid to the pan and gently simmer for 10 minutes.

3 Add the milk and bring the liquid back to the boil, stirring as you go. When it reaches boiling point, take it off the heat, add the tea, put the lid back on and allow it to infuse for around 4 minutes.

4 Strain into cups* and serve, sweetening to taste.

* Traditionally, Indians use small glasses known as 'cutting chai' – the smaller portion 'cutting the chai in half'.

Variations:
If you want even more spice in your chai, try adding a few extra ingredients such as some grated ginger, a bay leaf, a pepper corn or two, or a few fennel seeds.

BLACK TEA CHOICE

We think masala chai works best with a robust black tea – Assam being our preference. This recipe makes a fairly mild and milky chai, so you could easily add another 1–2 tsp of tea if you want something stronger.

Genmaicha

Genmaicha is a Japanese blend of green tea and toasted rice that has proved to be one of our favourite brews. There is a theory that the rice was originally added to bulk out the green tea and make it a cheaper drink, but our Japanese Tea correspondent* suggests it was developed as a way of adding a good aroma to any green teas lacking in the olfactory department. The tea is also called 'popcorn tea' as some of the grains are prone to popping (like popcorn), providing a potential bit of kitchen amusement for anyone making it.

Makes: 1 cup
½ cup white rice
½ cup green tea

* *Nagahiro Yasumori of Horaido Tea Shop. It was Master Horaido who first came up with the idea for the blend in the 1920s.*

** *The Japanese also blend un-browned white rice with tea, but they use it more sparingly, because when they look in the pot the white rice reminds them of the tea plant's flowers, and a good tea plantation has very few flowers.*

*** *You will have to listen for a lack of bubbling water to know if it has dried out. Or use a transparent lid.*

Although 'genmai' means 'brown rice', it's white rice you'll need for this recipe – the roasting turns it brown.** We've had success with basmati and long grain rice but for authenticity get hold of some Japanese rice (often referred to as 'sushi' rice).

1 Before roasting you need to steam or boil your rice, and before that you have to remove as much starch as possible so the grains don't stick together (which is a particular curse with Japanese rice). Soak in cold water for 10 minutes then rinse until the water runs clear.

2 Next, boil or steam your rice. If you have a preferred method, use it, if not try the following: place the rice in a pan with the same volume of water plus a third. Put the lid on and slowly bring to a boil. Turn down and simmer for 10–15 minutes (or until there is no water left). Turn off the heat and let it stand for a further 10 minutes. Resist the temptation to lift the lid throughout.***

3 When cooked, give the rice a shake in a sieve to drain off excess water and spread the grains on a plate to cool and dry. If they're still a bit stuck together, then another shake in a sieve when dried should separate them. Spread them out on a non-stick tray or one lined with greaseproof paper and roast them in an oven at a temperature of 200°C (400°F) until golden brown. This is likely to take around 25 minutes.

4 Allow the rice to cool, then combine with your green tea at a 50/50 ratio and use 1 tsp per serving. This tea is best brewed at a temperature slightly below boiling point, so switch off the kettle before it boils or leave the water to stand for a few minutes before pouring.

Turmeric Latté

Turmeric latté, often referred to as 'golden milk', has grown rapidly in popularity over the last few years, initially migrating from Asian kitchens to trendy cafés before becoming a relatively common sight on drinks menus in all types of establishments. As with all fashionable recipes, everyone will have their own theory on how best to make it and ours is based on simplicity. Whisk one up first thing in the morning or last thing at night and bask in its soothing golden glow.

Makes: 1 cup
1¼ cups of milk
1 tsp freshly grated (or
    1 tsp ground) turmeric
½ tsp freshly grated (or
    5 tsp ground) ginger
¼ tsp cinnamon
Honey or maple syrup,
    to taste

1 If you have fresh turmeric and ginger roots then grate them finely into a small pan, otherwise ground powder is fine. Add the cinnamon – either crumbled from a stick or already ground.

2 Fill your chosen cup with milk, pour it into the pan, then add the remaining quarter to allow for evaporation. This is a great recipe for trying out milk alternatives, with coconut milk and almond milk being our favourites.

3 Slowly heat the mixture, giving it an occasional gentle whisk to disperse the spices. Turn off the heat just before it boils and give it a final quick whisk, putting a bit more vigour into it than during the earlier stages – this will give your latté a pleasantly frothy texture.

4 Pour into your cup (straining it if you've used fresh ingredients), sweeten with honey or maple syrup to your desired taste and, if you want to give it an extra visual flourish, a sprinkling of cinnamon on the surface will look the part.

PEPPER POWER

Some people add a pinch of black pepper to their lattés to make them healthier. Turmeric contains curcumin (responsible for its colour), which is claimed by some people to be an antioxidant and antibacterial, but it isn't very good at absorbing into the body. Piperine, which is found in pepper, is said to aid curcumin's absorption; and thankfully, pepper's spicy notes aren't going to ruin your golden milk.

Roasted Barley Tea

Barley isn't the most obvious crop to grow on a small scale, but a patch of allotment that Rich gives over to cereal produces enough to make a few bottles of beer and several pots of this tea. It's a popular beverage in Korea where it's known as *boricha* and is served hot or cold. We've never visited Korea so can't compare it to a locally brewed cuppa, but our attempts have produced a pleasing nutty, toasty drink that's a bit like beer but without the booze.

Makes: 1 cup
3 tbsp barley
400 ml (14 fl oz) water
1–2 tsp honey, to taste

1 You can buy pre-roasted barley or you can use regular barley and roast it yourself – we've found pearled barley works the best. To create the desired roastiness either heat it in a heavy bottomed pan or skillet over a medium heat for 5–10 minutes, regularly tossing and turning the grains, or lay out on a tray and put in a hot oven preheated to 200°C (400°F) and bake for about 15 minutes. They're ready when they take on a deep golden colour (too much roasting unleashes less appealing burnt flavours).

2 To make the tea, put the roasted barley into a saucepan and fill with water.

3 Bring the water to a boil then cover with a lid and allow to simmer on a low heat. We find 15 minutes does the trick but you can leave it for longer if you want a more intensely flavoured drink, or just 10 minutes for a lighter brew.

4 If you have a sweet tooth then 1–2 tsp of honey perfectly complements the nutty goodness of this beverage.

5 Strain the liquid into a mug and serve hot or chill it for a cold caffeine-free alternative to iced coffee.

Sun Teas

Sun teas are one of summer's treats and involve your chosen ingredients slowly infusing their flavours into water by the power of the sun alone. It's a simple, fuss-free process: just put your ingredients into a jug, fill with water and set aside in a sunny spot. Within a few hours you'll have a flavoursome drink that can be enjoyed straight from the jug or chilled in the fridge.

This slow method of brewing rewards you with drinks that have slightly different characteristics to teas that use boiling water, with lighter, cleaner and fresher flavours. Start them in the morning and they'll be ready for lunch, making a great feature of a shared meal with friends. You can even top up the jug with more water as you go. Over the next four pages we've got three of our favourite sun tea recipes, but part of the fun in making them is strolling around the garden and filling a jug with whatever takes your fancy – so let the summer sun send your imagination wild.

A SIMPLE LEMON SUN TEA

This sun tea is as basic as it gets and allows you to appreciate the flavours of a slow, low-temperature tea infusion with just enough lemon to give it some citrussy freshness.

Makes: 1.2 litres (2 pints)
4 black tea bags
½ a lemon
1.2 litres (2 pints) cold water

1 Put the teabags into a jug with the lemon (squeeze the juice into the jug before adding the rind). Fill with cold water and cover. If your jug doesn't have a fitted lid then use a clean tea-towel, clingfilm or alternative makeshift cover such as a plate.

2 Leave it to infuse for 2–3 hours before serving immediately or chill in the fridge for later.

PEACH AND RASPBERRY SUN TEA

If it's a good year for raspberries then there are times when we can't pick them fast enough, so a sun tea is great for a quick pick-and-brew on the more bountiful days. Tart raspberries love joining forces with sweet juicy peaches, and they're both happy in the presence of black tea, which makes this recipe one of our fruitiest favourites.

Makes: 1.2 litres (2 pints)
4 black tea bags
2 peaches, sliced
1 large handful of raspberries
2 slices of lemon
1.2 litres (2 pints) cold water

1 We choose not to grow peaches so rely on the greengrocers instead, squidging our fingers through their boxes to seek out the ripest and juiciest specimens, because nothing short of perfectly ripe will do for this brew. When satisfied with your peachy haul, wash them, slice them and chuck them in a jug.

2 You also need ripe raspberries – throw them in whole following a thorough rinse. Add the black tea bags, slices of lemon and top up with cold water.

3 Cover the jug and set aside to infuse for 2–3 hours before drinking or putting in the fridge for later. This recipe benefits from a good stir before serving so grab a long-handled spoon and rattle it around the liquid with some determination. Strain into glasses and serve with ice and a slice of lemon.

TROPICAL HIBISCUS SUN TEA

Hibiscus flowers could be made specifically for sun teas. Not only do their tart, fruity flavours make perfect summer supping, but you also get the added visual bonus of the tea steadily reddening over time until it reaches a deep crimson hue. In this caffeine-free recipe we've ramped up the tartness a notch with lime – some fruits are cagey about releasing their full flavour in an infusion, but just a small amount of lime juice will add a lip-smacking sourness to this tropically refreshing mix.

Makes: 1.2 litres (2 pints)
2 handfuls of dried hibiscus flowers
1 handful of fresh mint leaves
¼ of a lime
1 thumb-sized lump of ginger
1.2 litres (2 pints) cold water

1 Drop the dried hibiscus flowers into a jug. Grab the fresh mint leaves, scrunch and tear them a bit to start releasing their minty oils then add them to the jug.

2 Squeeze the lime juice into the jug.* Follow it with the juiceless chunk of rind.

3 Roughly chop the ginger and give it a bruising to help release its sweet spicy flavours – a pestle or the blunt end of a heavy knife are suitable implements. Drop these pieces into the jug and add the cold water.

4 Cover the jug and set aside to infuse for 2–3 hours before drinking or putting in the fridge for later. Strain into glasses and, if you're the kind who likes a garnish, then a sprig of mint or slice of lime should suffice.

A NOTE ON QUANTITIES

It's not worth getting too hung up on precise quantities for sun teas. The jugs we use tend to be around 1.2 litres (2 pints) capacity, so our quantities will suit this volume, give or take a splash or two. You can also make single cup sun teas by filling smaller jars with a fraction of the ingredients.

ARE SUN TEAS SAFE?

Search for sun teas on the internet and it won't be long before you'll find an article questioning their safety – this is because the sun can heat your mix to a temperature that encourages bacteria growth from tap water and foodstuffs that would otherwise be killed off by boiling water. To minimize risk, you can use purified water and make sure the ingredients are thoroughly clean before using them, infuse for no more than three hours in a cooler location and get the resulting tea in the fridge if you're not going to drink it immediately. If you're the extremely cautious type then 'cold brew' instead – fill the jug with all the ingredients and infuse overnight in the fridge.

* If you like extra-sour drinks, by all means add another quarter or two to the mix.

SWEETENING YOUR SUN TEA

We tend not to sweeten sun teas, but if you need your hit of sugar then you're best off adding it in liquid form so it can dissolve into the blend. Runny honey or a syrup should do the job nicely.

Boozy Teas

Tea isn't a drink to be simply enjoyed in its own right, it also makes a useful ingredient for numerous other beverages, especially alcoholic drinks.

BEER AND TEA: A WINNING COMBINATION

Tea and beer may seem like an unusual combination, but tea from the *Camellia sinensis* plant has a lot in common with hops – it provides flavour, aroma and bitterness – so perhaps it's not so surprising that various types of teas have been included in beer recipes. Similarly, many of our wild tea ingredients have found their way into beery brews, so we figured one of our favourite blends, The Thirsty Gardener Tea (see *page 127*), might make a decent beer.

In order to test this theory, we hopped down to Cornwall to meet Brewing Manager Rob Orton at the world renowned St Austell Brewery, who helped us make a beer for real. In order to work out which hop varieties would work best with the lemon verbena and green tea, and to figure out what quantity of each to use, our first task was to brew up a tea with those key flavouring ingredients – a common practice among brewers when conjuring up any new recipe.

But brewers get to enjoy another hot beverage before the hops and other flavouring ingredients are added. When malted barley is first mashed to extract the sugar and flavour from the grains, a small amount is poured out to gauge its sugar content. This hot, sweet liquid is similar to other malted barley drinks and is known as 'brewer's breakfast', with the lucky brewers getting a mugfull to see them through the morning.

The final tea-making duties occur once the beer is fully fermented. If it's felt that the beer needs a flavour boost, then another tea is made from the same ingredients used in the brewing process, and this is added to the cask during conditioning. If our results are anything to go by, tea and beer are indeed a winning combination.

COCKTAILS

These days the fashion for fancy cocktails sees bartenders using all sorts of ingredients to help create their own unique recipes, and teas are becoming one of the most popular additions around. But the use of tea in boozy mixes isn't new. A drink known as gunfire, which consists of a simple combination of rum and black tea, has been enjoyed by the British Army since the nineteenth century, while hot toddies have long been made with black tea (see our recipe below).

You can also have fun inventing cocktails with one of your own wild teas – perhaps a mint tea mojito; an elderflower iced tea combined with the botanical flavours of gin; or even a dandelion coffee in an espresso martini.

And it's not just cocktails that have been enhanced with a drop or two of tea – tea can also be fermented to make a sparkling soda, kombucha (see *page 160*) or even wine.*

Think of tea as simply another flavouring ingredient and there are unlimited options for making a wild and wonderful boozy brew.

OUR HOT TEA TODDY

This winter warmer will banish any sign of the sniffles.

Makes: 2 cups
500 ml (16 fl oz) water
2 tsp lemon juice
2 cloves
1 cinnamon stick (around 10 cm/4 in in length)
1 star anise, lightly crushed
2 cm (¾ in) piece of root ginger, peeled and roughly chopped
2 tbsp honey
1 tsp black tea (or 1 tea bag)
3 tbsp brandy

1 Put the water, lemon juice and spices into a saucepan and warm gently over a low heat.

2 After a couple of minutes add the honey and stir until dissolved.

3 Continue heating for 10 minutes, giving it the occasional stir for good measure. Switch off the heat and add the tea and brandy and allow them to infuse for 2 minutes, giving the mixture another good stir or two to tease out more flavour.

4 Remove from the heat and pour through a strainer into heat-resistant glasses or mugs.

* *Makers of country wines (elderflower wine, parsnip wine, and so on), often put black or green tea into their mix to give the resulting booze the kind of tannic crispness you would normally get from grape skins.*

GREEN TEA AND CUCUMBER MARTINI*

You can make a simple wild tea martini by combining any flavoured spirit (see below) with vermouth. We suggest starting out with this simple and refreshing green tea and cucumber infusion.

For the green tea and cucumber vodka
200 ml (7 fl oz) vodka or gin
2 tsp green tea
1 piece of cucumber around 5 cm (2 in) in length

For the martini
60 ml (2 fl oz) infused vodka or gin
15 ml (½ fl oz) vermouth
Ice
Cucumber slices, to garnish

1 You can use gin or vodka for this infusion, but make sure it's a decent one and, if you've opted for gin, use one that hasn't been flavoured by other dominant ingredients. The classic martini uses dry vermouth but we think this recipe also lends itself to a sweet vermouth.

2 To flavour your spirit of choice, slice or chop the cucumber into small cubes and add to a lidded jar with the vodka and green tea.

3 Seal the lid, give it a vigorous shake and set aside for 20 minutes. Strain the liquid into a separate jar or bottle.

4 To make the martini, first fill a cocktail shaker with crushed ice. Add the infused vodka and vermouth. Stir for 30 seconds (or shake if James Bond is your guest) and strain into a cocktail glass. Eschew the tradition of garnishing with an olive, or even a twist of lemon peel, and instead add a slice of cucumber.

SPIRITS

A great way of introducing wild tea flavours into other drinks is to infuse them in spirits. Many of the ingredients in this book will be suitable and the spirits' high alcohol content will quickly get to work extracting the flavours. As a guide, gin lends itself to herbal and floral teas; vodka is a great base for punchy fruit flavours; and some of the spicy chai blends work a treat in dark rums. Quantities and infusing times will vary greatly according to ingredient, but start with small quantities of spirits and tea, taste-test at regular intervals, and have fun experimenting to see what works the best.

* Rich wants to call this a Mar-TEA-ni. Nick isn't so sure.

Strawberry Iced Tea

If you're the kind of person who gets excited by the sight of strawberries, then this summertime tea might just set you off on berry frenzy. It's a quick and easy brew that doesn't require any syrup making – simply pick, blend, chill and revel in the sweet taste of strawberry.

Makes: 1 litre (1¾ pints)
1 litre (1¾ pint) water
4 tsp black tea or 4 black tea bags
8 tsp sugar (or more for a sweet tooth)
Juice of ½ a lemon
500 g (1 lb 2 oz) fresh strawberries, plus a few more, to serve

1 Boil 500 ml (16 fl oz) water and pour it over the tea and sugar, stirring to dissolve the sugar, and let it stand for 5 minutes.

2 Meanwhile, hull and roughly chop the strawberries, place in a blender and blend until smooth.

3 When the tea has steeped, strain it into the blended strawberries, give it a stir and strain them through a fine sieve. For maximum juice extraction, try pressing the mix with the back of a spoon to force it through the tiny holes.

4 Add the lemon juice and a further 500 ml (16 fl oz) cold water then place in the fridge to chill. Stir before serving, adding ice to your glass and garnishing with a few slices of fresh strawberries.

STRAWBERRY TEA VARIATIONS

Minty Strawberries
Strawberries are one of mint's many admirers. Scrunch up a small handful of fresh leaves (or 2 tsp of dried leaves) and add to the tea.

Strawberries and Cream
Strawberries also love vanilla, and for a cream tea without the cream you can add ½ of fresh vanilla pod (or 1 tsp of vanilla essence) with the teabags. If you're desperate for the dairy as well, try floating a scoop of ice cream on the top.

Extra Fruity
For an even fruitier iced tea, add some more soft fruit to the strawberries, such as a handful of fresh raspberries.

Apple Scraps Tea

We live in an area that is famed for its apples and we grow several varieties ourselves, principally for cider making. This tea is for more sober supping and makes a handy bonus for anyone baking a big apple pie who finds themselves with a mound of leftover apple peel and cores. Apples have varying amounts of tannins in their skins, which gives the tea a refreshing bite, while boiling brings out every last drop of fruity flavour and sugar. It's also a great tea to make with kids who will enjoy transforming curly peels into a tasty drink. Although this recipe works perfectly well with apples alone, it can also be brewed with a flavour partner — we've picked out a few of our favourites for you to try, but why not have some fun and come up with your own ap-peeling combinations.

Makes: 2 cups
Peel and cores from
   5 medium-sized
   apples
800 ml (1 pint 4 oz)
   water
Brown sugar, honey or
   maple syrup, to taste

1 Pour the water into a pan along with the apple peel and cores and, if you wish, one of the optional additions.

2 Bring the pan to a boil and simmer for 10–15 minutes.

3 Strain into a mug and sweeten to taste – sugar or honey are suitable but we can also recommend a teaspoon of maple syrup.

OPTIONAL ADDITIONS

Fiery apple
Roughly chop or grate a small thumb-tip-sized knob of ginger and add it to the pan.

Fruity apple
Try boiling the mix with around 10 blackberries or raspberries.

Spicy apple
Add ½ a cinnamon stick to the pan with the apple scraps.

Minty apple
Pop 5 mint leaves into a mug with the hot liquid.

TOP TIP

Every time you peel an apple, pop the peelings in the freezer ready for when the apple tea mood strikes.

Elderflower and Cucumber Iced Tea

The sight of elderflowers spreading their creamy white blankets of blossom across a sunlit hedgerow is a sure sign that summer is making its entrance. Those elderflowers make one of the best iced teas around and, in this recipe, we've cooled the temperature down even further with the addition of cucumber. Clear space in the fridge and load up on one of the best tastes of summer.

Makes about 1 litre (1¾ pints)
12 heads of hand-sized elderflowers
Juice of 1 lemon
1 litre (1¾ pints) water
½ cucumber, plus extra, to serve
8 tsp sugar (or more for a sweet tooth)
4 tsp green tea (or 4 green tea bags)

CUCUMBER GARNISHES

For an alternative garnish, try using borage flowers or the young leaves of salad burnet, both of which have a distinctive cucumber-like flavour.

1 First give your elderflower heads a shake and rinse to remove any tiny bugs, then separate the flowers into a heatproof bowl – snipping with scissors or rubbing them off between finger and thumb are both suitable methods. A few tiny stalks joining them is fine, but as they contain bitter toxins you don't want too many creeping in. Add the lemon juice.

2 Bring 600 ml (1 pint) of water to the boil, pour it over the elderflowers, cover and leave overnight.

3 The next day, peel half a cucumber and roughly chop into chunks. Put the sugar into a pan with 400 ml (14 fl oz) water and bring to the boil, stirring to dissolve the sugar.

4 When the water has reached boiling point, take it off the heat and add the cucumber. Let this sit for 2 minutes so that it cools slightly, then add the green tea and allow it all to infuse for a further 10 minutes.

5 Combine the cucumber and green tea mix with the elderflower mix and strain it all into a jug (you'll need a fine sieve or muslin cloth for this task). Refrigerate for at least 1 hour until chilled.

6 To serve, you can add slices of cucumber and mint leaves as a final flourish of freshness before enjoying the coolest of summer drinks.

Kombucha

A sweet and sour fizzy tea sounds wrong on many levels, but this probiotic beverage of uncertain Eastern origin can provide a great platform for your wild tea experiments. It's produced by adding a live yeast culture called a scoby* (also referred to as a mother) to a sweet tea mixture. The scoby will then snack on the sugary tea, producing a small amount of alcohol and lending the beverage a light sparkle. The following recipe describes how to make a basic black tea kombucha, but you can use whatever tea blend takes your fancy, just as long as at least a quarter of the blend is black tea. Leaf through the pages of this book and let your imagination run wild.

Makes: 2.3 litres (3½ pints)
2.3 litres (3½ pints) water
4 tsp black tea (or black tea mix)
200 g (7 oz) sugar
scoby
350 ml (12 fl oz) starter tea
Note: You can use tap water but it really depends on where you live and the quality of the water supply. Water that has been chlorinated may inhibit your scoby growth, so to play it safe, either use bottled water or boil and cool tap water before use.

Equipment
3 litre (5¼ pint) glass jar
1 cloth for covering the jar
1 funnel or syphon tube for transferring your kombucha into bottles.

SCOBY AND STARTER TEA

To make your very first batch of kombucha, you'll need to get hold of a scoby. Either source one from a kombucha-making friend or search online – health food shops may be able to point you in the right direction. A 'starter tea' is usually an amount of liquid taken from your previous batch of kombucha, but shop bought scobys should come supplied with a pre-made starter tea.

METHOD

1 Bring 1 litre (1¾ pints) of water to the boil then turn off the heat and add the black tea.

2 Allow to steep for 5–10 minutes, strain, then add the sugar and stir until dissolved.

3 Add the sugary tea to a 3-litre (5¼-pint) jar and top up with 1.3 litres (2¼ pints) of cold water – ensure there is at least 5 cm (2 in) clear at the top for the starter tea and scoby and extra space for fermentation activity. Cover and allow to cool to room temperature.

4 Add the scoby and the starter tea. Give it a stir with a wooden spoon. Cover the jar with a cloth and secure with an elastic band. Keep the jar somewhere warm, but out of direct sun – a kitchen shelf is ideal.

5 Wait for 7 days, then taste. If your brew tastes too sweet, cover it and continue fermentation so that the sugar content continues to reduce. By 3 weeks your kombucha should have peaked and will taste tart.

* Or SCOBY – often written in capitals as it is an acronym for Symbiotic Culture Of Bacteria and Yeast. We've kept it lower case, as we didn't want you to think we were shouting.

SCOBY HOTELS

Once introduced to your kombucha, your scoby will expand, grow and form new scobys. Separate and transfer these to a 'scoby hotel' – a jar containing kombucha liquid where your scobys can live happily. Every month or so, you'll want to discard some of the liquid and top it up with sweet tea (see steps 1 and 2). Don't refrigerate it or allow your scobys to dry out, and discard any scobys that have turned black.

6 When the kombucha has reached your desired taste, lift out your scoby and either place it in a scoby hotel (see above) or immediately set it to work on your next batch.

7 Using the funnel or syphon tube, transfer your kombucha into sterilized swing-top bottles, leaving 1–2 cm (½–¾ in) of headspace.

8 For further customization, you can add additional flavourings to each bottle. Try adding a fruity syrup, some fresh herbs, or a couple of tablespoons of crushed or chopped fruits, such as strawberries.

9 Leave the bottles at room temperature for 1–3 days. A secondary fermentation will start to occur that will bring added sparkle to your drink. Release any excess CO_2 build-up by popping the caps on your bottles once daily.

10 Store your finished kombucha in the fridge to chill before drinking. It should keep for 1–2 months.

Bubble Tea

You could be forgiven for thinking that this quirky beverage was born of the Instagram generation, but Bubble Tea is no fleeting modern fad. It sprang up in Taiwan in the 1980s and has slowly gained worldwide popularity thanks to the numerous, customizable flavour combinations it offers, and the addition of boba – either chewy tapioca pearls or popping spheres of juice or syrup. For the experimental tea-maker looking for something a bit different, this tea and tapioca tryst provides the ideal canvas for wild creations.

BUBBLE TEA BASICS

Bubble tea can essentially be broken down into three basic styles, with each one offering up plenty of opportunities for customization. Follow the rough quantities given right and adjust the milk/tea ratios to your preferred taste. If you prefer a lighter, fresher brew, swap out black tea for green tea.

PLAIN BUBBLE TEA

Makes: 1 cup
1 cup of cold black tea or
   flavoured iced tea
1 lemon slice
3–4 ice cubes

Combine and shake vigorously to blend before filling with the boba of your choice.

MILK BUBBLE TEA

Makes: 1 cup
1 cup of cold black tea
½ cup milk (or milk substitute,
   see *pages 24–25*)
3–4 ice cubes

Combine and shake vigorously to blend before filling with the boba of your choice.

NOTE

Some of the more acidic fruity additions may curdle your milk depending on which type you choose. Citrus fruits are especially guilty of this. If curdling occurs, either swap the syrup, forgo the milk or simply suck it up.

FRUITY BUBBLE TEA

Makes: 1 cup
1 cup of cold black tea
Fruity syrup to taste
   (see *page 166*)
3–4 ice cubes

Combine and shake vigorously to blend before filling with the boba of your choice.

BOBA ADDITIONS FOR BUBBLE TEA

To provide that all important texture, just add boba. The two most common types are tapioca pearls and the slightly more labour intensive popping boba. Here's how to make them:

TAPIOCA PEARLS

Although it's possible to make your own tapioca pearls from scratch, we'd recommend purchasing a pack of dried ones. Search for them in your local Asian supermarket. Failing that, venture online where you will find plenty of willing vendors.

Makes: 1 large cup
1 cup of tapioca pearls
10 cups of water
Honey or syrup, for sweetening

To prepare them, add your pearls to a pan of boiling water (you'll need 10 cups of water for every cup of pearls) and wait until they rise to the surface. Give them a stir and continue to boil for 2–3 minutes before turning down the heat and simmering for a further 2–3 minutes. Scoop out the tapioca pearls, plunge them in cold water for 20 seconds then drain. Mix the pearls with honey or syrup for sweetening and flavour before adding to your cup of bubble tea.

DID YOU KNOW?

Tapioca pearls are made from an extract derived from the roots of the cassava plant, a woody shrub native to South America. Care must be taken when preparing the cassava plant for processing (which should involve peeling, slicing then cooking) as raw cassava contains a naturally occurring cyanide.

POPPING BOBA

It's a bit more bothersome to make popping boba, but the end results are worth the effort. This 'reverse spherification' technique involves encasing your chosen syrup or flavouring with a gelatinous membrane that bursts when bitten into. The ingredients are best sourced online.

Makes: 1 large cup
1 litre (1¾ pints) distilled water
5 g (¼ oz) sodium alginate
100 g (3½ oz) syrup of your choice (see *page 166*)
2 g (⅔ oz) calcium lactate
Xanthan gum (optional)

1 Grab a mixing bowl and pour in 1 litre (1¾ pints) of distilled water, then add the sodium alginate.

2 Using a blender, whisk for 5–10 minutes then leave to cool in a fridge for around 30 minutes to ensure that the alginate hydrates properly.

3 In a separate bowl, pour in the syrup and add the calcium lactate (and xantham gum, if using, see step 4). Stir vigorously to combine.

4 Carefully drip blobs of the mixture into the alginate bath using a spoon or a large syringe from a height just above the surface of the bath. Stir the newly formed spheres around carefully with a slotted spoon, then after 30 seconds, transfer them into the rinsing bath.

Your first attempts will most likely look like Satan's frogspawn, but with a bit of practise you should be able to make decent spheres. If you keep getting odd-shaped boba, your flavouring mixture may need thickening. To fix this add a small amount of xanthan gum in step 3 until the mixture is viscous.

FOUR EASY-TO-MAKE
GARDEN-FORAGED SYRUPS FOR BUBBLE TEA

Here are four fruity syrups to incorporate into your bubble tea experiments. You can also use them to splurge over ice-cream and they make great cocktail additions to a gin and tonic or a similarly summery, spirit-based concoction.

WOODRUFF SYRUP

Folks familiar with the insides of German beer halls will probably have spied this syrup accompanying a Berliner Weisse, to which it adds a straw-like sweetness. Green food colouring is often added to woodruff syrup to give it a punchy green hue.

Makes: 1 bottle
1 bunch of sweet woodruff
600 ml (1 pint) water
300 g (10 oz) caster sugar
2 lemons, washed and sliced
Green food colouring (optional)

1 Wash the woodruff, pat it dry and allow it to wilt for a day or so to intensify the flavour.

2 Add the water and sugar to a saucepan and bring to the boil. Reduce the heat and simmer to dissolve the sugar, then allow to cool.

3 Pluck the leaves from your woodruff and add them to the pan. Add the sliced lemons, then cover and chill for a couple of days in the fridge.

4 Strain the syrup through a muslin cloth. Return it to a pan and bring to the boil, then remove from the heat. Allow it to cool before pouring into sterilized bottles, adding food colouring if you like.

ROSEHIP SYRUP

This is without question one of the finest wild syrups you could ever hope to make. Pour it in your tea, pour on pancakes, or just glug it neat like a filthy animal.

Makes: 1 bottle
500 g (1 lb 2 oz) rosehips (roughly chopped)
600 ml (1 pint) water
300 g (10 oz) caster sugar
Juice of 1 lemon

1 Mash up your rosehips using a mortar and pestle or similar, then place in a saucepan along with the water. Bring to a boil, then simmer for 15 minutes.

2 Remove from the heat, then strain through a muslin cloth into another pan. Give it an encouraging squeeze if need be.

3 Strain again through a clean muslin cloth to ensure no irritating rosehip hairs make their way into the final syrup.

4 Add the sugar, then bring to a boil, stirring until the sugar has dissolved. Continue to boil for 5 minutes more, skimming off any scum that rises with a spoon.

5 Pour into sterilized bottles when cool.

TOP TIP

When kept refrigerated, your syrups should last for a month or so. Give them a shake before use if the liquid has started to separate. Adding 1 tsp of vodka when bottling will extend their shelf life to around 6 months.

RHUBARB AND GINGER SYRUP

Don't just save it for crumble, turn your rhubarb stash into a pink-hued syrup for your bubble tea experiments. Mix with tapioca pearls and a slice of vanilla pod for a bubble tea take on rhubarb and custard.

Makes: 1 bottle
500g (1lb 2oz) rhubarb stalks
600ml (1 pint) water
Juice of 1 lemon
300 g (10 oz) caster sugar
1 knob of fresh ginger, grated

1 Chop the rhubarb into 2.5-cm (1-in) chunks and place in a large pan, along with the water, lemon juice, sugar and ginger.

2 Bring to the boil and simmer for around 30 minutes, until the rhubarb turns pulpy.

3 Remove from heat and strain through a muslin cloth into another saucepan or suitable receptacle. You might need to squeeze the bag a little to encourage the juices to flow but beware that the bag and contents will be HOT. Suspend the bag and let it drip for a few hours if possible.

4 Pour into sterilized bottles when cool.

LEMON BALM SYRUP

This tart, lemon-flavoured syrup is just the ticket for summertime slurping. Give this one a go with a base bubble tea made from chamomile instead of black tea.

Makes: 1 bottle
600 ml (1 pint) water
300 g (10 oz) caster sugar
1 large handful of lemon balm leaves
Juice of 1 lemon

1 Add the water and sugar to a saucepan and bring to the boil, stirring until the sugar has dissolved. Reduce heat to a simmer.

2 Add the lemon balm leaves and lemon juice and continue to simmer for around 10 minutes.

3 Strain through a muslin cloth and pour into sterilized bottles when cool.

Wild Coffee

For a wild alternative to the UK's favourite pick-me-up, head outdoors with your finest foraging bag and get gathering. The nuts, roots and seeds on this page offer surprisingly tasty 'real' coffee alternatives, packed with slightly bitter, roasted flavours and provide instant success without the alarming price tag. The only real difference is the lack of caffeine – which can be a bonus or a curse, depending on which way you look at it.

DANDELION COFFEE

Who would have thought that the roots of this tenacious lawn-loving plant could produce such a tasty brew? You shouldn't have much trouble sourcing willing plants – a quick trip to our unkempt allotment will often yield enough to make a tray-load of steaming beverages.

Serve: 1–2 tsp per cup

1 Dig up your dandelion roots, scrub and leave to dry on a warm windowsill.

2 Break or chop up your roots into small pieces.

3 Roast on a baking tray for 30–40 minutes at 200°C (400°F) until brittle, then grind them up with a pestle and mortar if you have one (a rolling pin/bowl combo will work just as well).

4 Use 1–2 tsp per cup of boiling water. Allow to infuse for 5 minutes before straining and serving.

CLEAVERS COFFEE

Cleavers (also known as goosegrass or sticky willy) make a fine coffee substitute. We'd argue that it tastes even better than dandelion coffee, albeit much more hassle to harvest. You'll also need to gather quite a lot – the plant-to-seed ratio is stacked considerably against the latter and it's the hairy seeds that you need. The resulting brew smells just like a freshly ground coffee – the taste is a kind of black tea/coffee crossover.

Serve: 1–2 tsp per cup

1 The best way to gather cleavers is to grab handfuls of the plant – stem and all – and allow it to dry out overnight. The seeds will then detach more easily from the stalks.

2 Spread a thin layer of seeds on a baking tray and roast for 20 minutes at 200°C (400°F).

3 Grind them up the best you can with a pestle and mortar.

4 Use 1–2 tsp per cup of boiling water. Allow to infuse for 5 minutes, then strain and serve.

ACORN COFFEE

Acorn coffee was used as a substitute during World War II when supplies of the real thing were scarce, and rumour has it that unscrupulous coffee makers would cut their stocks with this nutty alternative to boost profits. Compared to dandelion coffee, acorn coffee is a bit of a faff to make as acorns are fiercely bitter and need boiling first to tame the tannins. It's still worth a go though if you happen to stumble upon a glut of nuts.

Serve: 1–2 tsp per cup

1 Pile your acorns in a pan, cover with water and bring to a boil before simmering for 15-20 minutes.

2 Allow to cool, then remove the hard outer shells with a sharp knife, taking care not to slice your fingers.

3 Roast on a baking tray for 30–40 minutes at 200°C (400°F) until brown and fragrant.

4 Chop your roasted nuts in a food processor before returning them to the oven for a further 20 minutes at 200°C (400°F).

5 Give them a final grind with a pestle and mortar.

6 Use 1–2 tsp per cup of boiling water. Allow to infuse for 5 minutes before straining and serving.

CHICORY COFFEE

Not to be confused with the leafy bitter vegetable of the same name, this coffee impostor is made from the roots of the blue-flowered herb *Cichorium intybus* – a close relative of the dandelion. Camp Coffee, the bottled coffee-flavoured syrup, is made using chicory and became popular during the 1970s when real coffee prices soared due to crop-spoiling frosts in Brazil.

Serve: 1–2 tsp per cup

1 Tug up your chicory, separate the roots from the plant, scrub and set aside to dry.

2 Break or chop up your roots into small pieces.

3 Roast on a baking tray for 30–40 minutes at 200°C (400°F) until brittle, then give them a good old grind using a mortar and pestle.

4 Use 1–2 tsp per cup of boiling water. Allow to infuse for 5 minutes before straining and serving.

Hazelnut Latté

We both studied at Coventry School of Art and Design in the early 1990s – innocent days before Starbucks or Costa had crashed the scene, and when coffee served in the city centre precinct came in two types – black or white. Asking for a hazelnut latté back then would have resulted in quizzical looks and guffaws, but nowadays you'll often hear its name barked at baristas in hipster coffee shops. Hazelnut syrup (the crucial ingredient) is readily available in most supermarkets, but we think our homemade recipe knocks them into a cocked hat. For that authentic coffee shop vibe, drink it from a paper cup with your name spelt incorrectly down the side.

Syrup
150 g (5 fl oz) hazelnuts, blanched and roasted (see boxout)
250 ml (9 fl oz) water
2 tbsp honey
150 g (5½ oz) light brown sugar

Latté
Makes: 1 large mug
Strong black coffee and milk (dairy or non-dairy, see *pages 24–25*)

TO MAKE THE SYRUP

1 Wrap your hazelnuts in a clean kitchen towel or plastic bag and pummel them into small pieces using a rolling pin or suitably heavy implement.

2 Pour the water in a pan, bring to a boil then stir in the honey and brown sugar until dissolved.

3 Add your smashed nuts, turn down the heat and simmer for 15 minutes. Stir occasionally so they don't burn on the bottom of the pan.

4 Strain the resulting mixture through a muslin cloth or sieve into sterilized bottles. It's good practice to allow liquids to cool sufficiently before pouring into glass bottles as they may crack. Plus there's a good chance you'll scald your hands on the lava-hot liquid. Store your filled bottles in the fridge.

5 Don't bin the leftover nuts – use them to top your morning bowl of porridge for a nutty bonus.

TO MAKE THE HAZELNUT LATTÉ

1 Half fill a mug with a strong black coffee of your choice (see *pages 168–169* for some foraged alternatives).

2 Top up with warm milk.

3 Add 2–3 tsp hazelnut syrup (or to taste).

4 Enjoy!

HOW TO BLANCH AND ROAST HAZELNUTS

500 ml (16 fl oz) water
150 g (5 fl oz) hazelnuts
2 tbsp bicarbonate of soda

To rid your hazelnuts of their bitter, papery skins you'll need to blanch them as below.

1 Preheat oven to 180°C (350°F).

2 Bring 500 ml (16 fl oz) of water to the boil in a saucepan, plunge in your hazelnuts and add the bicarbonate of soda. Boil on the hob for around 4–5 minutes.

3 Remove from the heat, strain the nuts in a colander and rinse thoroughly in cold water. They'll look like a big pile of rotten molars, but don't let this put you off.

4 Remove the skins from the nuts by rubbing them with your fingers. Once they've come off, rinse again under cold water and dry them with a kitchen towel or similar.

5 Place your skinless hazelnuts on a baking tray and roast them in the oven until golden brown, which should take around 15 minutes.

6 Stand back and admire your lovely nuts. Store them in an airtight container for up to 6 months.

HARVESTING HAZELNUTS

Hazelnuts (also known as cobnuts) should be ready to harvest in late summer or early autumn. Although they are best picked when ripe, you'll often find that squirrels will have gotten there before you have a chance to fill your foraging bag. Beat them to it by picking the nuts while still green and storing them to ripen. Keep them inside a cardboard box somewhere dark, warm and dry like an airing cupboard. Store them for a couple of weeks, giving the box the occasional shake, and wait until the nuts separate readily from their cases. Remember to remove the outer shell before use.

Blackberry Frappé

Here's our wild take on a Greek frappé, the frozen frothy coffee designed for summertime supping. It's a beverage that requires a spot of vigorous mixing – we use a cocktail shaker for style and swagger, but novice baristas may want to err on the side of caution. A shaker packed with frappé can lead to unexpected kitchen spillages, so to prevent a Greek tragedy, pay attention to the boxout opposite.

Syrup
500 g (1 lb 2 oz) blackberries, stalks removed
400 ml (14 fl oz) water
200 g (7 oz) caster sugar

Frappé
Makes: 1 large mug
200 ml (7 fl oz) strong black coffee or coffee substitute (see *pages 168–169*), chilled
100 ml (3½ fl oz) milk of your choice (see *pages 24–25*)
4–5 ice cubes
1 generous scoop of soft vanilla ice cream
3 tbsp blackberry syrup
Whipped cream, to serve

TO MAKE THE SYRUP

1 Put your blackberries into a pan, add water and bring to a boil.

2 Put a lid on the pan and simmer for 30 minutes, or until the fruits have turned into a mush. To give them a helping hand, mash them with a potato masher.

3 Remove from the heat then strain through a muslin cloth into a pan. It may take a while for the pulpy mix to give up its juice, so suspend the bag and let it drip if you can.

4 Once all of the juice is in the pan, add the sugar, give it a stir and bring to a boil.

5 Stir until the sugar is dissolved. Continue to simmer for 5 minutes then set aside to cool. Pour into sterilized bottles; it will keep for about 1 month in the fridge.

TO MAKE THE BLACKBERRY FRAPPÉ

1 Pour the coffee into a cocktail shaker, along with the milk, ice cubes and ice cream. Add the syrup (use more or less, depending on taste).

2 Give it a vigorous shake for 30 seconds, until the ice is smashed and the milky coffee is foamy.

3 Pour into a large glass and add a straw. Top with a dollop of whipped cream if that's what takes your fancy.

OUR TOP TIPS ON COCKTAIL SHAKING

1. Shake it Firmly

Hold your shaker with both hands, one supporting the base and one gripping the neck, with fingers curled firmly over the lid.

2. Shake it Hard, Shake it Long

Don't be shy, give it some welly! Look to shake for around 20 seconds. If you are using a fancy stainless steel shaker, the outside will form frost, letting you know the contents are ready for pouring.

3. Shake it Safe

If you have been ignoring step 1 and the lid of the shaker flies off, shaking over your shoulder will ensure that your guests aren't showered in frappé. Speaking from experience, blackberry frappé doesn't wash out of clothes all that well.

Index

Acknowledgements

Big thanks to everyone who helped us make this book happen, in particular Dave Hamilton for his expert foraging advice and Jane Moore at The Bath Priory for her growing know-how and the photo opportunities her immaculate garden provided. We would also like to thank our foreign correspondents Nagahiro Yasumori, Natsuki Kikuya and Wendy Dewar, as well as those who supplied invaluable knowledge closer to home – Sue Mullet of Bath Botanicals, Meghan and Rob at St Austell Brewery and the good folk of St Ives Gin.

Thanks to our agent Jane for connecting us with Lisa Dyer at Eddison Books, who has been full of advice and encouragement, and everyone else involved in the production of the book, including Nicolette Kaponis, Grace Paul, Anna Cheifetz, Ruth Jenkinson (photography) and James Pople (design). Other people we would like to mention for their assistance and support are Becky, Liz and Lenny, Emman Depau and Lyndsey Mayhew.

Finally, Rich would especially like to thank Catherine, Daisy, Emily and Annabel and Nick has oodles of extra gratitude for Kerry and Flynn – all for helping us to pick, brew and taste. We promise to never again ask you to try mallow tea (although we can't promise there will be no more stinky seaweed experiments).